Perceived Leadership Style and Job Satisfaction: Analysis of Instructional and Support Departments in Community Colleges

Perceived Leadership Style and Job Satisfaction: Analysis of Instructional and Support Departments in Community Colleges

Dr. Ruben Johnson

Copyright 2014

A Dissertation Presented in Partial Fulfillment
Of the Requirements for the Degree
Doctor of Management in Organizational Leadership

University Of Phoenix

ISBN: 1514224984
ISBN 13: 9781514224984
Library of Congress Control Number: 2016915473
CreateSpace Independent Publishing Platform
North Charleston, South Carolina

The Dissertation Committee for Ruben Johnson certifies approval of the following dissertation:

PERCEIVED LEADERSHIP STYLE AND JOB SATISFACTION: ANALYSIS OF INSTRUCTIONAL AND SUPPORT DEPARTMENTS IN COMMUNITY COLLEGES

Committee:

Christopher Van Ness, Ph.D, Chair
J. Paul Gallagher, Ed.D, Committee Member
Neil Mathur, DBA, Committee Member

Jeremy Moreland, PhD
Academic Dean, School of Advanced Studies
University of Phoenix

Date approved: December 9, 2014

Abstract

The purpose of this quantitative descriptive correlational study was to measure the relationship between the subordinate's perceived style of leadership of their leader and the subordinate's level of job satisfaction while assigned to various instructional and support departments within one of the North Texas community college districts. The job satisfaction of the employees of the instructional and support departments within a community college is a necessity for the survival of the educational institution. The foundation of job satisfaction is based on the professional relationship established between the leader and their subordinates, and whether or not the subordinates are satisfied with their jobs. The participants in this study completed two survey instruments: Multifactor Leaders Questionnaire, 1995 or MLQ-5x (see Appendix E) and Minnesota Satisfaction Questionnaire, 1967 or MSQ (see Appendix G), and a Demographic Questionnaire (see Appendix D). The current study results suggested the relationship between the perceived leadership styles (independent variables - transactional, transformational, and laissez-faire) and overall job satisfaction (dependent variable) for the employees who worked in the instructional and support departments. The current study results indicated a sufficient relationship between the MLQ-5x sub-categories of both transformational and transactional leadership styles and job satisfaction (MSQ) in both departments.

The results indicated a negative relationship between laissez-faire leadership style and job satisfaction in both departments. In addition, the findings of the current study have leadership implications for college administrators, managers, supervisors, and the subordinates.

Keywords: community college, job satisfaction, leadership, perceived leadership

Dedication

I hope this study will encourage leaders to learn more about their style of leadership and how it impacts the job satisfaction and productivity of their subordinates, while serving in a community college environment.

I dedicate this dissertation to my mother, Gloria E. Gary (Irizarry), who passed away in October 1992. Mamma, I love you and thanks for the opportunity that you gave to me while on earth to give hope and encouragement to others who are less fortunate than me. May God be with you until we meet again.

"But without faith, it is impossible to please him; for he that cometh to God must believe that he is, and that he is a rewarder of them that diligently seek him."
HEBREW 11:6.

Acknowledgements

First and foremost, I thank God Almighty for the opportunity and the ability that he granted me to complete this dissertation in lieu of my challenges and setbacks. I thank my wife, Demetriss A. Johnson, for her unconditional love and ongoing support during the long nights and weekends. I thank my children, Angellica M. Johnson, Gabrielle M. Johnson, and Tre A. Beacham for their love and putting up with me while I strived to accomplish this goal. Thanks goes to my brothers, Ivan L. Johnson, Anderson L. Johnson, and Willie E. Johnson and their families, for their love and support as I strived to accomplish this goal.

Special thanks to my administrative assistants, LaTasha Adams, Leah Durham, Sandie Harcourt and Shellye Lyons, who constantly reminded me to set aside time to write, edit, and then write some more. I appreciate the support and understanding provided by my colleagues at Cedar Valley College (Executive Deans - Dr. Mickey Best, Dr. Rabarb Fares, Jennie Pollard, and Lisa Nightingale) and the entire Dallas County Community College District.

I express my deepest appreciation to my mentor, Dr. Christopher Van Ness, who provided guidance, hope, and a swift kick when I needed it. Dr. Van Ness' guidance was timely, clear, and consistence. Also, I appreciate the encouragement and direction given by my committee members, Drs. J. Paul Gallagher and Neil Mathur. Without their timely feedback, this dissertation would not have been possible.

Many thanks go to my peers and friends, Drs. Betty Hearns, Robin Washington-White, Tuesday Hambrick, and Sheila Lamar for their continuous push and inspiration. Special thanks to Russell Haynes, who challenged daily not to quit.

Special thanks to my pastor, Dr. Rodney D. Dulin, and church family at the Central Pointe' Church of Christ for their prayers, encouragements, and well wishes. Also, I want to give special thanks to Brother David L. Chandler, Rodney E. Craft, Christopher B. Crear, Duane L. Johnson, Jerome Madison, James D. Mitchell, Demetrice Sanders, and Willie J. Tucker, and their families for their continuous faith in me to complete this task.

Special thanks to Drs. Jennifer Wimbish, Wright L. Lassiter, Zena Jackson, Elsie Burnett, and Nancy Cure' for the part they played in help making my research to become a reality. I also want to thank my statistician and colleague, Mathewos Kassa, for helping me to understand the steps of collecting the data and presenting it in a meaningful manner. I truly appreciate everyone who had a hand in helping my dream to come to fruition.

The influence of one's circle is a powerful instrument.

Table of Contents

List of Tables

List of Figures

Chapter 1

● ● ●

Introduction

A s the economy of the United States continues to fluctuate, different bud-
gets allocated to the federal, state, and local academia institutions (universities, colleges, high school, secondary, and elementary) will become more
reduced and scrutinized (Altundemir, 2012; Grummon, 2010). The reduc-
tion in allocation of educational funds forces administrators of each institution to streamline and evaluate their hiring process, retention, and job
satisfaction level of their departmental managers and subordinates (Frick,
2011; Hargis & Bradley, 2011; Schweer, Assimakopouls, Cross, & Thomas,
2012). In addition, due to future budget constraints and the sustainability of the institutions, specifically, community college administrators must
do a better job of retaining critical managers and subordinate employees to
serve in various staffing capacities in the instructional and support departments within the local college (Gnage & Drumm, 2010; Riggs, 2009; Vega,
Yglesias, & Murray, 2010).

As organizations investigate ways to hire managers and subordinates, the
institution and leaders must also look for new or different methodologies to
ensure employee job satisfaction is a priority and receive equal attention as
hiring and training. Despite the importance of the selection process, organizations tend to hire individuals as leaders who do not possess the essential knowledge, competency, or skills necessary to direct their departments

or divisions (Eichinger, 2007). The failure to hire quality leaders may lead to employees being unhappy with their managers and dissatisfied with their jobs, thus producing weak or poor outcomes in their daily job performance. Some hired leaders lack the necessary social skills and do not fit within the organization's culture. The development of a leader in social intelligence and interpersonal skills could be beneficial to the organization by enhancing subordinate productivity and organization commitment (Bambacas & Patrickson, 2008). Benefits to the organization may include an increase in its overall performance, establishment of effective relationships with external partners from other organizations, and a positive rapport between the manager and employees due to job satisfaction and a high level of job performance (Norris, 2009).

Chapter 1 introduces an overview of the current study on how the subordinate perceived the style of leadership of the leader and how the subordinate's perception determine the level of job satisfaction of the employees from the instructional and support departments within one of the North Texas community college districts. The current study may be of significant to leadership because the study addresses how the leader's style of leadership can influence the operation of a work section or department within one of the North Texas community college districts. This chapter also provides the background, problem statement, purpose statement, the significance of the current study, nature of the study, research question, hypotheses, theoretical framework, definitions, assumptions, scope, limitations, delimitations, and a chapter summary, as they relate to perceived leadership style and job satisfaction.

Background of the Problem

In any organization, most leaders are considered as the subject matter experts (Gregory-Mina, 2009; McCall & Hollenbeck, 2008). Leaders are expected to make things happen. According to Cordeiro (2010), hiring the right individual for management is vital to the accomplishments of any organization regardless of the vision, mission, strategy, or discipline. The ideal candidate should be one who understands, supports, and promotes the mission of the organization. Recently, there has been an enormous amount of discussion regarding employee turnover rates by various businesses and educational institutions, especially community colleges needing to fill leadership positions (Basham, Stader, & Bishop, 2009; Reille & Kezar, 2010). The American Association of Community Colleges (AACC) predicted approximately 75% of the senior management in the community college environment would retire in the twenty-first century (McNair, Duree, & Ebbers, 2011; Strom, 2011). Because of this expected wave, colleges across the United States find themselves fighting for top leaders from a small pool of qualified applicants to fill these positions (McNair, Duree, & Ebbers, 2011).

In 1995, the University of Florida's Department of Education leadership hosted the Community College Futures Conference. The conference participants pointed out the main issues confronting community colleges as follows: (a) creativity and small business ownership is critical for survival, (b) hiring and retaining of the right employee, (c) emphasis on goals and strengths, and (d) creation of teams (Basham, Stader, & Bishop, 2009). The current study will focus on item (b): hiring and retaining of the right employee to fill the future leadership and subordinate positions. To improve retention rate of employees, upper management must understand and address the concept of *employee satisfaction* (Freed, 2006; Ratna & Chawla, 2012). Barrick and Zimmerman (2009) noted the common denominator for most turnover theories' is that some employees are more attached to their job and organization than others are. Job satisfaction was noted as one of the key forces which caused employees to stay on their jobs (Mansell, Brough, & Cole, 2006; Mochama, 2014). With this in mind, the researcher hopes to uncover how a leader's style of leadership (*transactional, transformational, and laissez-faire*) correlates with the subordinate's level of job satisfaction (*very satisfied, satisfied, neither satisfied nor dissatisfied, dissatisfied, or very dissatisfied*) within a community college environment.

The current study explored the leader's style of leadership under a specific focus. In this current study, the meaning of leadership includes the following three styles or factors: *transactional* (based on a reward system and punishments), *transformational* (based on inspiration and behavior charisma), and *laissez-faire* (based on non-leadership) (Kedsuda & Ogunlana, 2008). The leadership styles or factors (independent variables) used in the current study was measured by the Multifactor Leadership Questionnaire (MLQ-5x) (see Appendix E) developed by Bass and Avolio (2004). The results from quality leadership consists of three measureable factors: *effectiveness* (the leader's ability to accomplish the organizational mission and goals), *satisfaction* (the degree which the subordinates are pleased with the leader's behavior), and *extra effort* (the degree which the leader influences the subordinates to increase his or her desire to succeed and perform higher than normal) (Kedsuda & Ogunlana, 2008).

The Minnesota Satisfaction Questionnaire Short Form, 1977 (MSQ) (see Appendix G) survey instrument (Weiss, Dawis, England, & Lofquist, 1967), measured the level of the subordinate's job satisfaction (dependent variable) in the current study. When leaders possess the correct style of leadership, the subordinates are content with their profession, apt to function at a higher level of productivity, and desire to have a longer tenure with the organization (Silverthorne & Ting-Hsin, 2001). According to Abualrub and Alghandi (2012), when the dissonance factor (the individual's difference between perceived and preferred styles of leadership) was considered, the narrowly the individual perceived and preferred styles of leadership are, the individual will be more satisfied with his or her job.

Statement of the Problem

The general problem observed in this current quantitative study was the increasing absence of efficiency and proficiency in the leadership within the community colleges (Carlos & Luke, 2012; Sypawka, Mallett, & McFadden, 2010). The specific problems observed in this current study consists of (a) the leader's ability to know how his or her style of leadership was perceived by his or her subordinates (Bucic & Ramburuth, 2010; Washburn, 2012; Wu, 2009). And, (b) the leader's ability to know how the subordinate's perception of the leader's style of leadership impacts the subordinates' level of job satisfaction (Lockwood, 2008; Sullivan, 2012) within a community college environment. This current quantitative study was a correlational research design that explored the relationship between the department leaders' leadership styles (independent variables - *transformational, transactional, and laissez-faire*) and the level of job satisfaction (dependent variable) of the subordinates who report to them. The general population of the current study included specific leaders (vice presidents, deans, managers, faculty, and coordinators). The subordinates (executive administrator assistants, division secretaries, and other office staff personnel, known as professional support staff) are those who are employed by one of the seven community colleges (Brookhaven College, Cedar Valley College, Eastfield College, El Centro College, Mountain View College, North Lake College, and Richland College) of the Dallas County Community College District (DCCCD) located in Dallas, Texas.

Purpose of the Study

The purpose of the current quantitative study investigates two things: (a) the subordinate's perceived leadership style of the leader and (b) the level of the subordinate's job satisfaction. The quantitative method was appropriate for the current study because this method enabled the researcher to collect and use data from a specific population and sample to describe trends and explain the relationship among different variables found within the current study (Creswell, 2005). The application of the quantitative method was appropriate and feasible for the current study, because this type of method compares relationship between two or more variables (Forde, 2011; Tanoe, 2010).

The current study consisted of a correlational research design. The researcher planned to explore the degree of association or relationship of the independent variables (perceived leadership styles and departments) and dependent variable (level of job satisfaction) to determine if they are related or whether one can predict the other (Creswell, 2005). The independent variables for the current study included the leader's perceived styles of leadership (*transformational, transactional, and laissez-faire*). The dependent variable included the subordinate's overall job satisfaction.

The specific population group for the current study consisted of employees within instructional departments (academic vice presidents, academic deans, academic program coordinators, faculty, academic administrative assistants, and academic instructional associates). Employees within support departments (student services/support vice presidents, student services/support deans, student services/support administrative assistants, student services/support staff members and other non-instructional personnel) of the seven community college campuses (Brookhaven College, Cedar Valley College, Eastfield College, El Centro College, Mountain View College, North Lake College, and Richland College) in the Dallas County Community College District (DCCCD). The leadership styles or factors was measured by the Multifactor Leadership Questionnaire (MLQ-5x) (see Appendix E) survey instrument. The Minnesota Satisfaction Questionnaire (MSQ) (see Appendix G) Short Form survey instrument measured the level of the subordinate's job satisfaction.

The geographic location of the current study consisted of the seven community colleges within the Dallas County Community College District (DCCCD), located in Dallas, Texas. The seven community colleges (Brookhaven College, Cedar Valley College, Eastfield College, El Centro College, Mountain View College, North Lake College, and Richland College) are located in the North Texas region of the state. Since these colleges are located within the same district and geographic area, the organizational structure and operational practice were similar.

Significance of the Study

The significant of current study highlights the importance of the leader knowing how his or her style of leadership relates to the employee's level of job satisfaction. In addition, the current study explores why or how the organization would benefit overall when the leader's style of leadership produces a positive relationship or outcome, which may have a direct impact on the employee's level of job satisfaction while working with his or her staff (Papalexandris & Galanaki, 2009). The findings of current study are applicable to the field of leadership, organizational design and structure, perceived leadership of the leader, and the subordinate's level of job satisfaction, as they relate to leaders and their subordinates within the community college environment in the instructional and support departments. Strong leadership manifests itself through creating strong departments and organizations (Anonymous, 2009; Ashley, 2008). Effective leaders can produce positive results and transform the cultural climate within the college and various departments by establishing collaborative and meaningful agendas and inspiring others to pursue them (Bloomdahl & Navan, 2013; Strom, Sanchez, & Downey-Schilling, 2011; Sypawka, Mallett, & McFadden, 2010).

Significance to Academics

The research of the academic leaders' style of leadership and the effects the style may have on their staff in the community college environment was limited. Universities and colleges may have solid leadership at the chancellors, presidents, and vice presidents level, but, if all other leaders in the organization are not performing to an acceptable standard, the organization is bound to regress and experience various degrees of chaos, which in turn may adversely impact enrollment, retention, and student success (Gentry, Katz, and McFeeters, 2009; Riggs, 2009). From an academic environment, employee turnover costs the organization insurmountable amount of loss of talent, training, disruption, and budget (Rosser & Townsend, 2006).

The current research study was significant to the field of higher education because the study addressed the growing need for upper management in each college to attract, hire, and retain "*satisfied*" subordinates in each department of the community college, especially within the instructional and support departments (Saniewski, 2011; Wilson, 2010). As student enrollment grows in higher education, so will the need for departments to perform at a higher level of efficiency and proficiency (Sypawka, Mallett, & McFadden, 2010; Zeiss, 2010). According to Phillippe and Mullin (2011), a survey conducted by the American Association of Community Colleges (AACC) stated that the total increase in enrollment of community college students for Fall 2009 and

Fall 2010 were approximately 3.2%, which equates to appropriately 250,000 students. This study also noted that during eight of the last 10 years, across the United States, the enrollment at community colleges increased to nearly 8.2 million students (Philippe & Mullin, 2011).

The retention of satisfied subordinates are critical to the accomplishments and growth of the organization (Carlos & Luke, 2012; Saniewski, 2011; Sypawka, Mallett, & McFadden, 2010; Wilson, 2010). As noted by Gentry, Katz, and McFeeters (2009), leaders who work in the roles of senior educational leadership positions are also critical to the success of the institution. Due to budget constraints, administrators should work differently and realize that professional development training in the subject areas of leadership style, job satisfaction, and job performance is a necessity to create and maintain a productive organization (Nicolaidou & Petridou, 2011; Sirkis, 2011). The current study results may provide the opportunity for the creation of special professional development programs and organizations to assist both leaders and subordinate to improve their leadership and level of job satisfaction.

Significance to the Study of Leadership

The findings of the current study contributed to the field of leadership by helping senior management increase their level of awareness of how leaders may be more effective within their organization not because of what they know or have experienced. Leaders can increase their level of awareness by adjusting or improving their perceived leadership style while interacting with their subordinates and others throughout the organization (Bennett, 2009; Sabri, 2012; Soieb, Othman, & D'Silva, 2013). Leaders need to understand their role within the organization (Christopher & Matviuk, 2010). Leaders need to recognize the "*real*" power of perceived leadership and how the perceptions impacts the subordinate's level of job satisfaction and job performance in the workplace needed to sustain and carry the organization forward into the twenty-first century (Drew, 2010). The current study helps leaders eliminate barriers from the workplace, so the leaders can create an environment to help the subordinates to achieve the maximum level of job satisfaction.

In a study conducted by Kiger (2008), leaders must uncover new ways to eliminate barriers so his or her staff can be successful. The leader should then allow autonomy by getting out of the way and allowing subordinates to get the job completed and perform at a higher level than expected. This type of leadership was not about personnel psychology; instead, this type of leadership was about community processes, trust, and success. According to Hogan and Kaiser (2008), leaders need to create a trustworthy environment, accept difference of opinions, push for collaboration, and highlight how cooperation helps the organization perform better.

The findings of this current study assist leaders, regardless of their style of leadership, to become better listeners, communicators, and individuals who can determine when the true message in the workplace is unclear (Neufeld, Wan, & Yulin, 2010). The data and results from this study may empower leaders regarding of the difference styles of leadership to have a clearer understanding about employee's job satisfaction. In addition, leaders may see the value of developing a closer working relationship with their subordinates instead of treating them with empathy or lording over them (Kamarul, 2008).

Nature of the Study

The researcher in the current study used a quantitative, correlational method. The quantitative method was appropriate for exploring the relationship between transactional, transformational, and laissez-faire leadership styles (independent variables). The leadership styles were measured by the Multifactor Leadership Questionnaire (MLQ-5x) (see Appendix E) survey instrument (Bass & Avolio, 2004), and the employee's overall job satisfaction (dependent variable) of the subordinate was measured by the Minnesota Satisfaction Questionnaire (MSQ) (see Appendix G) survey instrument (Weiss, Dawis, England, & Lofquist, 1967). Creswell (2002) noted that quantitative research methods are appropriate for describing trends and exploring the relationship between the variables. In contrast, researchers use qualitative research methods to explore and understand a central phenomenon.

Research Method

The researcher selected the quantitative method because this method was best suited to address the research problem, research question, and to explore the relationships between the different variables (dependent and independent) (Azorin & Cameron, 2010). The correlational, quantitative research was suitable because the method demonstrates the strength of correlation existing between the pairs of variables. In a quantitative study, numeric data are collected using instruments developed prior to the research, so that reliability and validity can be established (Creswell, 2005).

Design Appropriateness

The correlational research design was appropriate for the current study because the design allowed the researcher to collect and use data from a specific population and compare professional relationships (Creswell, 2005). The current study explored the perceptions that the subordinates have of their leaders' transactional, transformational, laissez-faire leadership styles, and their level of job satisfaction in the instructional and support departments within a community college environment. Correlational studies are most valuable when they make forecasts about dependent variables and answering queries regarding relationship type activities (Creswell, 2005; Neuman, 2005). Qualitative research was not appropriate for the current study because the intent of the current study was not to investigate phenomenon of predictive and criterion variables (Arcidiacono, Procentese, & DiNapoli, 2009). The researcher implemented the correlational design for the current study because quantitative research methods required descriptions and explanations. The current study measured the correlation between *transactional, transformational, and laissez-faire* leadership styles and the level of job satisfaction by implementing a correlational design. The current study used the Multifactor Leadership Questionnaire (MLQ-5x) (see Appendix E) to assess the relationship of the leaders' leadership behavior styles and the Minnesota Satisfaction Questionnaire (MSQ) (see Appendix G) to evaluate the relationship of the level of job satisfaction of the subordinates. The MLQ-5x (Bass & Avolio, 1990) and the MSQ (Weiss, Dawis, England, and Lofquist, 1967) survey instruments are recognizes as valid research tools. The MLQ-5x and MSQ surveys were the primary instruments for collecting data from the known population.

Research Question

The current study explored one research question to determine what, if any, correlations existed between the leader's perceived style of leadership and the subordinate's level of job satisfaction. The following research question was used as the basis to answer the phenomenon of the different level of the employee's level of job satisfaction: What is the relationship between the subordinate's perception of the leader's style of leadership and the subordinate's job satisfaction level within the instructional and support departments in one of the North Texas community college districts?

Hypotheses

The first hypothesis was composed to address the relationship between the subordinate's perception of the leader's transformational style of leadership and the subordinate's job satisfaction level while working within an instructional or support department in one of the North Texas community college districts. The second hypothesis was composed to address the relationship between the subordinate's perception of the leader's transactional style of leadership and the subordinate's job satisfaction level while working within an instructional or support department in one of the North Texas community college districts. The third hypothesis was composed to address the relationship between the subordinate's perception of the leader's laissez–faire style of leadership and the subordinate's job satisfaction level while working within an instructional or support department in one of the North Texas community college districts.

Thus, the current study tested the following hypotheses:

$H1_0$: There is no relationship between the subordinate's perceptions of the leader's style (the degree to which a leader uses) of transformational leadership and the subordinate's job satisfaction level while working within an instructional or support department in one of the North Texas community college districts.

$H1_a$: There is a positive relationship between the subordinate's perceptions of the leader's style (the degree to which a leader uses) of transformational leadership and the subordinate's job satisfaction level while working within an instructional or support department in one of the North Texas community college districts.

$H2_0$: There is no relationship between the subordinate's perceptions of the leader's style (the degree to which a leader uses) of transactional leadership and the subordinate's job satisfaction level while working within an instructional or support department in one of the North Texas community college districts.

$H2_a$: There is a positive relationship between the subordinate's perceptions of the leader's style (the degree to which a leader uses) of transactional leadership and the subordinate's job satisfaction level while working within an instructional or support department in one of the North Texas community college districts.

$H3_0$: There is no relationship between the subordinate's perceptions of the leader's style (the degree to which a leader uses) of laissez–faire leadership and the subordinate's job satisfaction level while working within an instructional or support department in one of the North Texas community college districts.

$H3_a$: There is a negative relationship between the subordinate's perceptions of the leader's style (the degree to which a leader uses) of laissez–faire leadership and the subordinate's job satisfaction level while working within an instructional or support department in one of the North Texas community college districts.

Theoretical Framework

According to Johnson and Christensen (2012), the theoretical framework was a written document that summarizes the prior literature relating to the current study. Lu and Botha (2006) penned that a theoretical framework helps to fill the space of the subject based on a broad literature review. The current research resided under the following broad theoretical areas to help the researcher to explore the concept of job satisfaction: effect theory, dispositional theory, two-factor theory, hierarchy of needs theory, equity theory, and goal setting theory.

The researcher centered the current study on the theories and studies relating to perceived style of leadership and job satisfaction (See Figure 1.1).

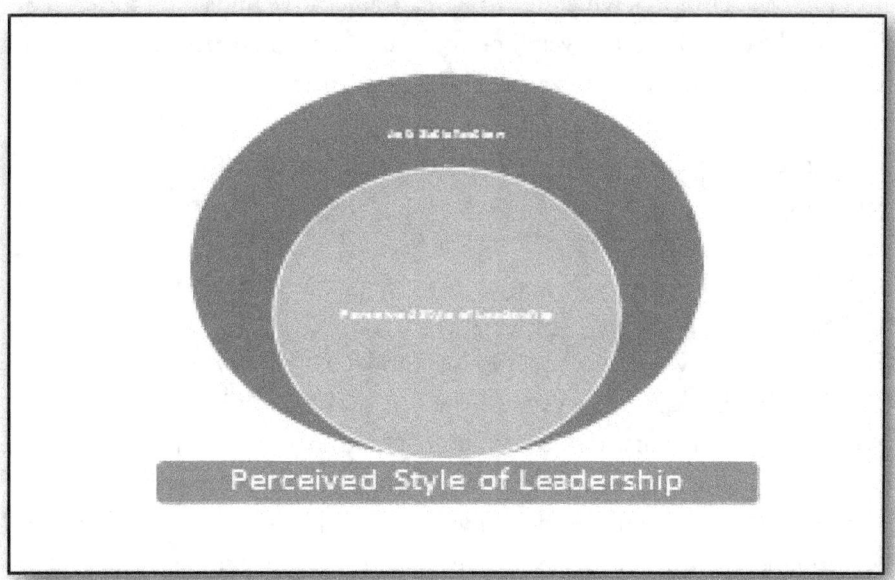

Fig 1. Johnson's Job Satisfaction Model

Bass (1990) stated that leadership was an instrument that helps organization accomplish goals and satisfy the organization's needs. Bennis (1991) penned that leadership was creative, adaptive, and agile. Leadership focuses on the future and not just on day-to-day activities. The primary mission of the leader was to define the mission and model behavior that encourages or influences the organization to move toward those goals. Effective leadership style(s) within an organization created an environment where job satisfaction of the employees leads to increased job performance, which also leads to increased productivity (Chitwood, 2010; Finn 2008).

Due to the expected shortage of high performing employees in the near future, organizations are encouraged to improve their hiring processes and train management groups to identify, award, and retain high-performing employees. The shortage of employees force the organization to revamp their human resource training program at general, leadership, and individual levels (Arms, 2012). The failure of organizations having a career succession plan causes a tendency for high-performing employees to become dissatisfied with his or her leader or job, which in turn create a negative impact on the employee's and the organization's overall performance in the marketplace (Valentine, 2011). As a result, the organization fail to meet their production and financial goals. Bass (1990) noted that the organization's mission, which consists of the purpose, objectives, and performance, correlates with the organization's leadership.

Overview

Effect Theory. The effect theory also known as the "law of effect" theory. The idea behind this theory states that an individual's job satisfaction can depend on two factors: the expectations a person has for a job and what a person was going to receive from the job. The smaller the gap between these two factors, the more likely the individual would be satisfied with his or her performance (Cohrs, Abele, & Dette, 2006). The effect theory also states that a person may flavor one aspect of the job more than another may and that certain aspects can relate to how satisfied the employee was. Behavior, which leads to negative consequences are not, repeated (DuBrin, 1997).

Dispositional Theory. Dispositional theory approaches assume that higher the temperament of an employee, the higher his or her job satisfaction (Cohrs, Abele, & Dette, 2006). Staw (2005) suggested that "a new dispositional model of job satisfaction was based on several informational and action steps including exposure to work events and condition, as well as the evaluation, memory, retrieval, and expression of affect in the organizational context" (p. 59). Bakotic and Babic (2013) noted that the dispositional effect, in some cases, includes earlier situational influences and earlier job outcomes.

Two-Factor Theory. The two-factor theory (motivator-hygiene theory), adopted by Fred Hertzberg, concludes that "certain job characteristics, labeled motivators, are more influential with respect job satisfaction, while other characteristics, labeled hygiene factors, are more strongly connected with job dissatisfaction" (Katz, 2004, p. 13). The basic underlying thought of this two-factor theory was the manager who works to improve the hygiene-type factors may succeed in reducing employee dissatisfaction. However, such efforts are necessary to increase the job motivation of employees. According to Pryor, Humphreys, Oyler, Taneja, and Toombs (2011), the extrinsic factors include such factors as pay, supervision, working conditions and job security. The extent to which extrinsic factors are absent (or not at an acceptable level) causes job dissatisfaction, but the presence of these factors above the acceptable level does not cause job satisfaction.

Hierarchy of Needs Theory. Abraham Maslow developed one of the most significant theories about an individual's need (Bolman & Deal, 2003). Maslow classified the needs of people into five basic groups:

1. *Physiological* – when an individual have the desires for air, water, nourishment, physical fitness, and relaxation.
2. *Safety* – when an individual have the need to feel secure from endangerment, violence, and intimidation.
3. *Belongingness and love* – when an individual have the need for positive and affectionate relationship with others.
4. *Esteem* – when an individual have the need to feel appreciated and he or she value themselves.
5. *Self-actualization* – when an individual need to develop himself or herself to the fullest and actualize his or her potential (Bolman & Deal, p. 305).

Bolman and Deal noted in Maslow's view, "once the lower needs are met or satisfied, individuals are then motivated by higher needs, such as belongingness, esteem, and self-actualization" (p. 305). The idea of needs "hierarchy" assumes that some needs are more essential than others are and they are satisfied before the other needs can serve as motivators (Schermerhorn, Hunt, & Osborn, 2008).

Equity Theory. Equity theory suggests that individuals experience distress when they perceives themselves as not being rewarded enough or too much and this concern leads to the desire and determinations to restore equity (Huseman, Hatfield, & Edwards, 1987). The equity theory includes four propositions:

1. People assess their associations by comparing with other individuals' outcomes and inputs.
2. If the results and contribution of others seen as imbalanced, then inequity exists.
3. The superior the inequity, the more distress.
4. The superior the distress, the more individual work to reestablish equity and decrease distress (Huseman, Hatfield, & Edwards, p. 222).

Goal Setting Theory. Organizations utilized goal setting for many reasons. Edwin Locke created goal-setting theory in the 1960's. The goal setting theory states that goal setting connects to task performance. The theory states that specific goals and appropriate feedback, contribute to better task performance (Kleingeld, van Mierlo, & Arends, 2011). In other words, goals indicate what need task to be accomplish and what activity and energy is necessary to complete the task. Scott (2003) noted that goals have five alternative functions: guiding, motivating, symbolizing, justifying, and evaluating behavior. The job characteristics model focuses on the job. The job characteristics model includes five features of a job, which affect an individual: skill variety, task identity, task significance, autonomy, and feedback or evaluation. These features of a job can influence the employee's perception and the significant of work. The fourth feature was autonomy; the more independence an employee experiences, the more a sense of responsibility will occur. The last feature is feedback or evaluation, which tells the employee how well he or she completes tasks (Cohrs, Abele, & Dette, 2006).

Definitions

The following definitions help provide a clear understanding of the terms used in the framework of the current study. According to Ramsey (2010), the definition of each term must be clear and understandable, as well as rigorous. The current study will include a description of how subordinates interact with their leaders in the workplace. The selected group of employees within instructional and support departments are located at the seven community college campuses (Brookhaven College, Cedar Valley College, Eastfield College, El Centro College, Mountain View College, North Lake College, and Richland College) within the Dallas County Community College District (DCCCD), located in the Dallas, Texas area.

Burnout: A state of being exhausted from repeated emotional stress of dealing intensely over a long period with other people (Corey & Corey, 2007).

Community College: The community college was "an ideal vocational education center because of its ability to expedite programs; its extensive geographic distribution across rural, suburban, and urban America; and its mission to serve local constituents of varying means, abilities, and motivations" (Ayers, 2010, para. 11).

Job Facets: A positive emotional response to specific job components (e.g., work itself, work conditions, pay, benefits, coworkers, supervisors) (Spector, 1997).

Job Performance: The behaviors and working results of staff (Chu & Lai, 2011).

Job Satisfaction: The employees' overall assessment of their professions and positive feelings toward their place of employment (Jex & Britt, 2008).

Leader: A leader or a manager is an individual person who leads the team (Rowe, 2006).

Leadership: Leadership includes the leaders' perception of the employee's trait, role relationship, perceptions, and the leader's traits, behavior, interactions, and the influence over the employees, task goals, and organizational culture (Yukl, 1989).

Leadership Style: Leadership styles or management styles are collectively learned behaviors that incorporate policymaking and the process of passing judgment, which includes goal-setting, strategic goals, and the implementation of the goals (Jain & Premkumar, 2010).

Subordinate or followers: The term subordinate or follower is one who reports or submits to another individual's authority, and he or she held responsible for his or her actions (Dixon, 2009).

Work Overload: Work overload are when individuals have long work hours and an unreasonable workload accomplished during an unreasonable timeframe (Altaf & Awan, 2011).

Assumptions

There were six assumptions that undergirded the current study. The first assumption is that the selected sample population who responds to the surveys may represent other typical employees (subordinates or followers) in other community college environments, or similar structured organizations, throughout the United States (Chesney, 2012). The second assumption is that the selected sample population would respond truthfully about how they perceived the leadership styles of their leaders. The third assumption is that the selected sample population would respond truthfully about how they evaluate their level of job satisfaction. The fourth assumption is that the selected population would respond truthfully about their knowledge and understanding of their own type of leadership style. The fifth assumption is that the selected population who respond to the survey and questionnaires would have a general knowledge about basic communication skills and concepts. The sixth assumption is that most leaders generally care for their employees and hope they are successful while working within and for the organization throughout their careers.

Scope, Limitations, and Delimitations

Scope

The scope of the current study included seven community colleges (Brookhaven College, Cedar Valley College, Eastfield College, El Centro College, Mountain View College, North Lake College, and Richland College) within the Dallas County Community College District (DCCCD), located in Dallas, Texas. The potential number of survey individuals of the target population was approximately 7,300 full-time and part-time employees who work within the instructional and support departments. The institutions chosen for this current study are two-year comprehensive community colleges that offer various associate degrees and a host of certificate programs.

The seven college institutions (Brookhaven College, Cedar Valley College, Eastfield College, El Centro College, Mountain View College, North Lake College, and Richland College) are located in Dallas County, in the North Texas region, of the state of Texas. Each institution offers classes traditionally on campus, on-line via the Internet, and hybrid, which is a combination of on-campus and on-line format. The researcher selected these institutions because of their similarity in organizational governance, they were located in the same district, and because the research may be conducted by a means of convenience sampling. In fall of 2012, the American Association of Community Colleges (AACC) recorded that there were a total of 1,132 community colleges (including 986 public, 115 independent, and 31 tribal) in the United States (AACC, 2012).

Limitations

According to Creswell (2005), limitations are possible weaknesses or problems in quantitative research recognized by the researcher. The current study was subjected to three limitations: (1) only individuals who agreed to participate on a voluntarily basis would be surveyed, (2) data collected from participants by means of self-reporting are known to potentially produce biased responses, and (3) the inability exists for the researcher to physically interview the participants face-to-face. The validity of the current study was restricted to the dependability of the survey instruments (MLQ-5x and MSQ) used in the current study.

Delimitations

The current study was limited to surveying both full-time and part-time employees (administrators, faculty, and support personnel) at the seven community colleges (Brookhaven College, Cedar Valley College, Eastfield College, El Centro College, Mountain View College, North Lake College, and Richland College) located within the Dallas County Community College District (DCCCD). The current study was limited to employees who worked in either the instructional or support department within one of the North Texas community college districts. The design of current research focus on those who were in leadership or managerial positions, and the subordinates who report to these leaders or managers. This current study did not focus on the students or the college's constituents in the local community because the current study deals directly with the workgroups in the local colleges to give their leaders and other decision makers a glimpse of how the employees' job satisfaction level related to the employee perception of the leader's style of leadership. Due to the limitation of time and other resources, only the employees of the seven institutions (Brookhaven College, Cedar Valley College, Eastfield College, El Centro College, Mountain View College, North Lake College, and Richland College) were included in the current research. Including other colleges in surrounding counties, such as Tarrant, Collins, and Johnson, would have brought about additional hardship for the researcher, and may have had a negative impact on the results of the current study.

Summary

Chapter 1 provided information on the major problems facing educational institution in the twenty-first century. Due to budgetary reductions, education institutions, specifically, community college administrators must shift their focus toward hiring, retention, and employee satisfaction. The purpose of the current study explored how employee's perceived leadership style impacts the level of the employee's job satisfaction. Employees tend to have higher level of productivity when the leader possesses the correct style of leadership and the subordinates are satisfied with their job (Bambacas & Patrickson, 2008; Norris, 2009).

Chapter 1 contained an overview of the current study on perceived leadership and job satisfaction. Chapter 1 also included the background, problem statement, purpose statement, the significance of the current study, nature of the study, research question, hypotheses, theoretical framework, definitions, assumptions, scope, limitations, delimitations, and a chapter summary as they related to perceived leadership style and job satisfaction.

Chapter 2 presents a review of the literature connected to the existing research in the field of perceived leadership and job satisfaction. The focus of the literature in Chapter 2 includes the following areas: introduction; titles searches, articles, research documents, and journal researched; conclusion; and a summary as they relate to perceived leadership style and job satisfaction.

Chapter 2

Review of the Literature

The goal of the current study was to determine the relationship, if any, between the subordinates perceived style of leadership of the leader and the subordinate's level of job satisfaction. Chapter 2 includes the current study's literature review, both historical and current findings, which exist in the fields of leadership, management, and job satisfaction that supports the research pertaining to the current study. The focus of the literature review includes seven areas: title searches, articles, documents, journals, research question, historical and current studies that relate to perceived leadership styles (transactional, transformational, and laissez-faire), and identifies the gaps based on the current study.

Title Searches, Articles, Research Documents, and Journal Research

The information obtained and researched by scholarly writers derived from an empirical origin to create validity and establish creditability about the topic and problem statement (Smith, 2008). Over 194 scholarly documents were used to research material for the independent and dependent variable(s) from the University of Phoenix electronic library databases (EBSCOhost, Thomson Gale Power Search, and ProQuest), dissertations, government documents, policy reports, national databases, professional societies, periodicals, industry surveys, private and public industries, peer reviewed empirical findings, scholarly journals, and scholarly textbooks (See Table 2.1). According to the Neuman (2003), the primary sources in which research findings are located in scholarly journal articles. Table 2.2 provides a synopsis of the literature reviewed in support of the related research areas.

Research terms used in the current study are "burnout," "community college," "job facets," "job performance," "job satisfaction," "leader," "leadership," "leadership style," "subordinate or followers," and "work overload."

Table 2.1

Overview of Major Literature Title Searches

Topic of Exploration	Peer-reviewed Studies
Community Colleges	178,908
Job Performance	134,482
Job Satisfaction	88,637
Laissez-faire Leadership	8,635
Leadership (general)	122,209
Leadership and Job Satisfaction (general)	55,944
Leadership and Job Satisfaction (suggested by ProQuest)	235
MLQ-5x	1,770
MLQ-5x and MSQ	56
MLQ-5x Colleges	1,371
MLQ-5x, MSQ, and Community Colleges	47
MSQ	876
MSQ Colleges	546
Transactional Leadership	10,390
Transformational Leadership	16,103

Table 2.2

Literature Reviewed in Support of the Related Research Areas

Types of Research Materials	Number Searched	Number Reviewed	Number Used
Peer-reviewed Journals	225	180	112
Researched Documents	45	36	31
Books	30	24	20
Totals	300	240	163

Research Question

According to Creswell (2005), research questions probe statements that reduce the purpose statement to precise inquiries that researches try to find in their studies. The conclusion of the current study will result in answering the following research question: What is the relationship between the subordinate's perceived style of leadership of the leader and the subordinate's level of job satisfaction within the instructional and support departments in one of the North Texas community college districts?

Purpose of the Study

According to Creswell (2005), the purpose of the research consists of identifying the major intent or objective for a study and narrowing the study into specific research questions or hypotheses. Creswell also noted that the purpose statement should contain the main emphasis, participants, and the location of the inquiry. The purpose of this quantitative study was to measure the relationship between the subordinate's perceived leadership styles of the leader (independent variables) and the subordinate's level of job satisfaction (dependent variable). The participants for this study will include the subordinates who work in the instructional and support departments for one of the seven community colleges (Brookhaven College, Cedar Valley College, Eastfield College, El Centro College, Mountain View College, North Lake College, and Richland College) in the DCCCD, located in Dallas, Texas.

Historical Overview

Job Satisfaction

According to Spector (1997), job satisfaction was determined when individuals like their jobs. From Spector's prospective, job satisfaction is classified in two areas: employee and organization. First, the employer should treat each employee fairly and with respect. Secondly, job satisfaction of the employees can have a positive or negative effect on the functionality of the organization. As the profitability of the organization from a global perspective becomes priority for many organizations, corporations are researching the correlation of job satisfaction and job performance (Chu & Lai, 2011). Spector noted that either people likes (satisfaction) or dislikes (dissatisfaction) their jobs because of various facets (see Table 2.3).

Table 2.3

Common Job Satisfaction Facets

Activity
Acknowledgment
Advancement opportunities
Associates
Business itself
Compensation
Establishment's rules and procedures
Fringe paybacks
Gratitude
Individual growth
Job settings
Management
Message
Nature of the work itself
Refuge

Source: Spector, P. E. (1997).

Leaders

According to Northouse (2010), leadership occurs when the leader influences the follower and the follower influences the leader. Leaders direct their energy toward individuals to achieve a common goal. Neither a leader nor a follower can act independently of one another. Bass (1990) noted that leaders play a mediating and connecting role between their followers and their own superiors. Bass continued by stating, successful leaders must have influence "upstairs."

In a study known as *exercise supervise,* Bass (1990) concluded that the greatest dissatisfaction of followers and leaders occurs when highly involved followers worked with authoritarian leaders, and the greatest satisfaction of followers and leaders occurred when highly involved followers worked with participative leaders (Bass, 1990). In the workplace, the leader and follower depend on each other to accomplish the mission. In addition, leaders and followers both give and receive benefits. In a transactional approach, the leader directs the group toward the common goal, and the followers provide the leaders with status (Bass). Bass suggested that the compliance of followers is the mirror image of successful leadership. The compliance of followers may appear as an instrument to the accomplishment of the mission, and both private and socio-emotional acceptance of the leadership effort.

Leadership

Allio (2013) offered advice to leaders by concluding that leadership, in general, materializes or improves over a period of time and instantaneously. At times, leadership appear and then disappear, because leadership is elusive. When leadership is active in the workplace, a number of things are changed, for example, the situation, the expectations of the subordinate, and the culture of the organization. Sutton (2010) noted that a manager's style of leadership influences the subordinate's level of performance as well as the level of the performance of the entire organization. Leader can enhance the performance of subordinates by showing confidence, avoiding indecisiveness, sharing recognition for good work, and accepting the accountability of their employees' performance (Sutton).

According to DeRue and Ashford (2010), leadership uniqueness is seem in the workplace when leaders and followers claim and grant their identities in social interactions with one another. DeRue and Ashford continued by acknowledging through the claiming and granting process, each person internalizes their identity by recognizing their roles within the organization. Hasan and Subhani (2011) noted, "there is a strong correlation between the social wisdom of the leader and the degree of employee turnover intentions, work commitments, and leader-employee relationship and wise leaders usually build long and valuable relationships with their employees and in turn transfer the managerial wisdom to others" (Hasan & Subhani, 2011, p. 132).

Kanji (2008) noted that leadership is accountable for driving the organization in the direction of or towards the area of quality and excellence. Taylor and Lynham (2013) defines leadership as "stewardship" and leadership continues to increased recognition of the ability to influence the trajectory of change. Leadership is best engaged to facilitate desirable outcomes. However, a number of work leaders state variations of leadership underdevelopment (Patel, 2013). The more researchers examine the concept of "leadership" the more researchers see that most concepts are simply techniques to support good person management. Workman & Cleveland-Innes (2012) submitted that genuine leadership is evident more in the results achieved than in the contributions used to obtain the results.

Leadership and leader are words that best refer to a person who has high morals, great speaking and writing skills, self-assurance, admired by others, and uses their conviction and inspiration to endorse collaboration and cooperation (Gaiter 2013). Leaders have the ability see in the future and the personality that others want to imitate. Leaders encourage change in others and they are not worried about failure. A leader must know him or herself before he or she can be an effective leader (Gaiter, 2013).

Leadership Styles

Usually, leadership styles are the techniques or the ways a leader provides direction, implement plans, and persuade his or her employees to accomplish the assigned task. The style of leadership tends to vary from leader to leader, based on his or her personality, research, emulation, experiences, employees, or situation (Riaz, Anis-ul-Haque, & Hassan, 2009; Stiefel, 2012). The style of leadership used by the leader is important, because the style determines whether the leader is effective or successful of aiding the team or organization to complete the goal. In the current study, the researcher will focus on three leadership styles: transformational, transactional, and laissez-faire.

Transformational Leadership Theory. Transformational leadership is the manner where leaders change subordinates into leaders. Transformational leaders stimulate challenge and build trust among followers (Avolio, 2011). Transformational leadership involves motivating others to go beyond what they initially planned and do more than they ever dream. "A person goes from doing a task for the money to doing the task because he or she identifies and takes pride in what is being produced" (Avolio, p. 15). Transformational leaders exhibit four major behaviors:

* *Idealized influence:* When leaders act as role models.
* *Inspirational motivation:* When leaders tend to motivate and inspire by challenging the work of others.
* *Intellectual stimulation*: When leaders encourage innovation and creativity by charging other to look at things differently and come up with different outcomes.
* *Individualized consideration*: When leaders observe each employees' needs for accomplishment and development (Avolio, 2011).

Transformational leaders are committed to changing the organization's level of motivation and confidence. According to Childers, Adams, Jaffe, and Briskin (2009), trust is the foundation for transformational leadership. Trust is the basic underpinning of leader and follower relationship. Warrick (2011) penned, "Nothing moves a group faster toward achievement, than having capable transformational leaders" (p. 11). Judge and Piccolo (2004) noted that transformational leaders focuses on higher-order, intrinsic needs. The transformational leadership theory implies leaders who optimize their power and influence (Cheung & Wong, 2011; Hearney & Gerbert, 2009).

Transactional Leadership Theory. A transactional style of leadership is the foundation for a more developed interaction between leaders and followers over time (Avolio, 2011). Transactions are the basis for building trust and identification and launching a sustainable, full-range leadership system (Avolio). Transactional leadership happens when employees are compensated or disciplined, based on their performance (Avolio). The transactional leaders exhibit three major behaviors:

* *Contingent reward* occurs when a leader ensures the employees know what needs accomplishing and the employed received proper rewards when the assignment is completed.
* *Management-by-Exception* takes place in form of remedial transaction and can be useless, predominantly when used too much.
* *Non-transactional or laissez-faire* occurs when there is absence of leadership (Avolio, p. 13).

Transactional leadership exist when something is exchange for something else that profits the leader, the employee, or both. Based on a study conducted by Groves and LaRocca (2011), "transactional leaders influence supporters by controlling their behaviors, rewarding agreed-upon behaviors and eliminating performance problems" (p. 512). Avolio, Bass, and Jung (1999) noted that the transactional leadership is the basis for building trust and the ideal of honoring of "contracts". Judge and Piccolo (2004) stated that transactional leaders concentrate their attention on the appropriate give-and-take of resources. Hamstra, VanYperen, Wisse, and Sassenberg (2011) noted in their study that transactional leadership encourages employees to complete their jobs strategically by obeying all rules, holding oneself and others responsible, avoiding mistakes, and sticking close to a concrete plan. Kezar and Eckel (2008) stated that transactional leadership incorporates control and exchange, political, and bureaucratic or structural theories of leadership.

Laissez–faire Leadership Theory. Laissez-faire leaders are "those who do not care what happens, avoid taking responsibility, cannot make up their minds, and are satisfied to sit and wait for others to take the necessary initiatives imposed by the task at hand" (Avolio, 2011, p. 263). Under the MLQ-5x study, laissez-faire leadership theory is the last category of leadership identified. The laissez-faire leadership is the evasion of leadership. Laissez-faire leaders are reluctant to make decisions and take corrective action (Valdiserri & Wilson, 2010; Stanford, 2014). Hinkin and Schriesheim (2008) noted that laissez-faire leadership shows leaders to lack stimuli response to a variety of situations. Laissez-faire leaders do not have the appearance of motivation or intention. According to Deluga (1990), "laissez-faire leadership implies leaders who are unwilling to influence subordinates" (p. 192). Subordinates are used to having an enormous amount of freedom.

Foster (2002) noted that laissez-faire (none) leadership style involves the leader allowing employees to take control and responsibility of all decisions and actions. However, in the article called *Successful Supervisor* (2012), the author penned that laissez-faire leadership style is appropriate when the workflow in the office is normal and slow. In a study conducted by Kanste (2008), laissez-faire leadership was positively associated with emotion exhaustion and depersonalization.

Effects of Good Leadership and High Job Satisfaction

The leader's actions and behavior usually set the tone in the workplace. The impact of good leadership by the leader and high job satisfaction by the employees leads to high collaboration; teamwork; creativity; enthusiasm; organizational commitment; productivity; self-valued; and increase number of goals attainment (Jernigan & Beggs, 2005). In addition, the impact of good leadership and high job satisfaction also leads to low absenteeism, mental illness, physical illness, and turnover (Amah, 2009).

Leaders are ambassadors of good leadership. A leader who emulate good leadership characteristics shows interpersonal sensitivity (attuned to his or her subordinates' thought and feelings) (Mast, Jonas, Cronauer, & Darioly, 2012). The more interpersonally sensitive the leader demonstrated the more satisfied the employees became. Ellis and Abbott (2013) penned that good leaders do not need to know how to manager, but a good manager of people is a good leader. Goslin (2012) noted that confidence, good communication, and good execution are important traits of a good (effective) leader. Subordinates receives positive energy when they feel (or know) they have the support of their leader.

Most employers desire to have jobs, which brings high job satisfaction to the employees. Mohr and Zoghi (2008) penned job satisfaction was connected to high-involvement in the workplace the participation in focus groups and suggestion teams by the subordinates. High job satisfaction contributes to subordinates who has a high commitment level, low absenteeism, high production, and low turnover rate (Rama & Nagini, 2013). High job satisfaction and high performance in the workplace can be tracked back to employee appreciation, recognition of performance, and the creation of bonding opportunities (Riordan, 2013).

Effects of Poor Leadership and Low Job Satisfaction

As leaders and organizations becomes aware of the cause and effects of the leaders' leadership and the employees' level of job satisfaction, the more the organization will be productive and the more the employees will be satisfied with their jobs. The impact of poor leadership and low job satisfaction leads to burnout; stress; high absenteeism; mental illness; and high turnover (Amah, 2009; Ram & Prabhakar, 2010). Also, the impact of poor leadership and low job satisfaction leads to low creativity; customer service; enthusiasm; morale; organizational commitment; productivity; and self-valued (Mor Barak, Travis, Pyum, & Xie, 2009).

Poor leadership is demonstrated when leaders do not perform the *right* (ethical) action(s) for his or her organization, co-workers, staff, and subordinates. Toxic leadership behavior of the leader can and will interfere with the attitude, moral, physical and mental well-being, and performance of others within the organization (Mehta & Maheshwari, 2013). The character of the leader often times set the tone for the standard of the organization and may impede the subordinates' level of satisfaction (Brookmire, 2007). Employees have the tendency to mimic what they hear and observe from their leader. Although, leaders are not perfect human beings, they must carry themselves as though they are walking a tight rope. Munby (2008) noted leaders should concentrate on building the perfect team, instead of being the perfect leader. Most leaders are proficient, experienced and virtuous in their behaviors, but some leaders are self-serving, conceited, and incompetent. Poor leadership hampers the workflow in the organization and cause damage that are irreparable (Mehta & Maheshwari, 2013).

Low job satisfaction experience by the subordinates can be attributed to somatic complaints, burnout, turnover, dissent, absenteeism, low or no supervisor support, and low financial reward (Thomas, 2002; Van Der Doef, Mbazzi, & Verhoeven, 2012;). In a study conducted by Loghmani, Golshiri, Zamani, Kheirmand, and Jafari (2013), some job satisfaction and discomfort may be associated with musculoskeletal symptoms. Mark and Smith (2004) confirmed that there might be some association to low job satisfaction to a person's well-being at work, which may also hinder their level of job satisfaction. The study conducted by Mark and Smith (2004) concluded that office stresses, intrinsic and extrinsic effort, and undesirable managing is associated with depression, anxiety, and low job satisfaction.

Job Satisfaction and Organizational Commitment

Organizational commitment comprises the employee's identification and participation with an organization (Tilleman, 2012). Due to today's highly competitive business organizations, companies must work hard to cultivate and maintain a productive workforce (Ansari, 2011). According to Ansari (2011), employees perceived three dimensions that correlate with their level of organizational commitment: fairness, effectiveness, and support. Although, there was positive correlation of all three dimensions, effectiveness and support were the most substantial predictors of organizational commitment. Riaz, Muhammad, and Hassan (2011) suggested that "the leader's style of leadership is one the determinants which influence the workforce commitment level" (p. 43).

Zeffane, Tipu, and Ryan (2011) noted companies are more interested in communication, trust, and organizational commitment within the organization. The research also suggests a substantial correlation between the usefulness of communication between the leaders and employees and organizational obligation, trust, and pride in working for the company (p. 77, para. 1). Zeffane, Tipu, and Ryan concluded that trust and organizational commitment do not just transpire; they are forged and preserved through effective communication (p. 77, para. 1).

As noted by Ekaterini (2010), the availability of opportunities for advancement and recognition determines the subordinate's job satisfaction and the level of his or her commitment. When commitment and opportunity are absent in the workplace, employees tend to become emotionally and mentally "withdrawn" from the organization (Ciftcioglu, 2011). Consequently, organizational commitment and job satisfaction are the key indicators of whether or not the employee is faithful to the organization. There are other studies by researchers that focus on job stress, high turnover, organization commitment, conflicts between management and employees, and job satisfaction in the workplace (Chu & Lai, 2011). The current study targeted the leader's influence of how the subordinate perceives the leader's leadership style and the impact on the subordinate's level of job satisfaction.

Community Colleges

The community college environment is the focus of the current study, but the research may be applicable to other organizations and industries. Therefore, regardless of the size, span of control, mission, or the configuration of the organization, the location of the current study applies to any organization. According to Mintzberg, Lampel, Quinn, and Ghoshal (2003), the environment is the various characteristics of an organization's outside context related to markets, political climate, and economic conditions.

The origin of the community college begins in the early nineteen hundreds. Like the university system, the community college system originally gave the faculty members a location to teach college level courses and work on various research projects (Morgan 2005). In 1901, the first community college, Joliet Junior College, originated in Joliet, Illinois. The community colleges provides affordable education to the public and acts as a pipeline to assist thousands who would otherwise have not succeed at the university level (Sullivan, 2010).

Since higher education training became a requirement for all professions, the need for community college system grew in demand (Sawyer, 2008). The number of community college institutions also grew in numbers because of active and prior service military personnel using Servicemen's Readjustment Act or GI Bill to pay for their college courses (Morgan, 2005). The need for community colleges continued to grow in the late 70's and 80's due the increased number of federal law bills which provided funding for workforce training in the various career field which experienced a shortage of personnel.

Today, community college offers the student the opportunity to complete their Associate degree or technical certificate in the career field of their choice. In addition, a student can attend the community college to earn his or her *core* courses (English, College Math, Liberal Art, and Science) approximately 42 credit hours, which enable the student to transfer from the community college to a university to acquire a Bachelor degree and move on to higher education. Morgan (2005) penned that the community college employees include not only full-time and part-time faculty members, but the institution also include administrators and support staff.

College structure includes division or department levels, with each department having a leader, often a dean, director, or manager (Sawyer, 2008). The dean serves as the administrator over the department. Each instructional department has an administrative office that provides administrative support, scheduling, faculty contract, and student support. Due to the college size, some institutions have associate deans, senior administrative assistants, and part-time staff to assist with the daily workloads (Sawyer, 2008).

MLQ-5x and MSQ Relevant Studies

There are many historical studies that have explored various findings as they relate to the leadership (MLQ-5x) (see Appendix E), and job satisfaction (MSQ) (see Appendix G) within various work environments. The MLQ-5x is a questionnaire used to measure transformational, transactional, and laissez-faire leaderships (Den Hartog & Van Muijen, 1997). The MSQ is a questionnaire used to determine the employee level of job satisfaction (Mardanov, Sterrett, & Baker, 2007). The following paragraphs provide the results of related studies:

Manufacturing Industry

In a job satisfaction study conducted with 250 employees at several electronic manufacturing facilities in Mainland China and Taiwan by Hsu (2007), the research noted a significant difference between the leader's perception of the managers' leadership style and the employees perceived the managers' leadership style. The study noted, "there was a significant difference between Mainland China and Taiwan in the perception of managers' transformational leadership style and employees' satisfaction of manager's leadership style" (p. 6). The research also noted there was a statistically significant difference in perception of intellectual stimulation and individual consideration for managers' leadership behaviors between Mainland China and Taiwan.

Detamore (2009) conducted a job satisfaction study with 1,392 employees of an engineering consulting firm. The study indicated that employees in an engineering consulting firm perceived their leadership as high in transformational leadership and low in laissez-faire style, which related to the firm's overall high levels of job satisfaction at both the facet level and overall job in general level, and low intent to leave. Both job satisfaction and perceived leadership style have linear correlations with intent to leave. For job satisfaction, the employees were very satisfied. Job satisfaction increases with tenure with the company and managers are more satisfied than non-managers are; however, all groups scored as being satisfied.

In a job satisfaction study conducted by Ozbaran (2010) of 196 Turkish traffic police officers of the Adana Police Department, the author suggested that officers were more satisfied when their immediate managers demonstrates transformational leadership behavior. The study did not find any correlation between other facets of job satisfaction (e.g., satisfaction with pay, coworkers, and opportunity for promotion) and the leadership styles of their immediate supervisors. The study also noted that the laissez-faire leadership style decreased the officer's job satisfaction.

Music Industry

In a job satisfaction study conducted with 390 respondents from 27 randomly selected orchestra conductors and musicians throughout the United States by Wood (2010), the study indicated a strong relationship to job satisfaction between transformational and laissez-faire leadership styles as the study relates to an orchestra musician. There was no relationship between transactional leadership and job satisfaction. The study also indicated no relationship between job satisfaction evaluations and musicians' occupation status.

Medical Industry

According to Long (2004), during a job satisfaction study conducted with 21 nurse supervisors and 179 nurses, nurses working for transformational leaders had the high level of satisfaction. Nurses working for laissez-faire managers had low level of satisfaction. The two lowest job satisfaction facets were pay and opportunities for promotion.

In another related medical job satisfaction study conducted by Chen (2005), with 175 Taiwanese nurse faculty members, the study indicated that Taiwanese deans and directors inclined to display transformational leadership more habitually than transactional and laissez-faire leadership in their place of work. In addition, Taiwanese nursing faculty members reported moderate levels of satisfaction in their jobs. The contingent reward, passive management-by-exception, and individualized consideration leadership styles were significant predictors of nursing faculty job satisfaction in Taiwan (Chen 2005, p. 85).

According to a job satisfaction study conducted by Hancock (2008), with 340 veterinarians of the Florida Veterinary Medical Association, the study indicated that transactional was a positively correlated with all facets. Leaders can improve both the transactional and transformational behaviors by improving job satisfaction by providing opportunities of pay and promotion. Hancock also noted that the study revealed that the transformational style leaders had a strong correlation to the work, promotion, and supervision facets of job satisfaction.

In a recent study, 54 community health workers in Texas, New Mexico, and California completed a survey. The study by Murillo (2008) indicated similar results from other existing studies; transformational leadership behaviors have a significant positive relationship with perceived managers' effectiveness. The study included correlations to the managers' effectiveness, transactional leadership and passive leadership mattered, but the relationship was not strong. Transformational leadership had a positive relationship with satisfaction, and supervision and passive leadership had an adverse relationship with satisfaction.

According to Gates (2009), who conducted a job satisfaction study with 62 full-time and part-time, home-based clinicians working with children who have developmental, emotional, behavioral, or other mental health needs, relationships suggested transformational leadership is the most useful when leadership wanted to hold on home-based clinicians. The study noted that "the correlations suggested that transformational style of leadership held a strong relationship with several underlying components of job satisfaction, which implied that this type of supervisory leadership style may be useful when trying to retain clinicians in the home-based setting" (p. 10). The study also provides the first step toward imagining how supervisor qualities *may* affect job satisfaction.

In a job satisfaction study conducted with 172 nurses in inpatient obstetric nursing in Illinois, purchased from National Certification Corporation, State of Illinois by Adebayo (2010), the findings indicated that transformational style has a resilient effect on employee perception of job satisfaction and organizational commitment. Transformational leadership behavior encourages employee productivity, job satisfaction, and organizational commitment. The study also noted that "there were three measurements of organizational commitment: (1) affective commitment (AC), (2) continuance commitment (CC), and (3) normative commitment (NC)" (p. 11).

In a job satisfaction study conducted by Ezeabasili (2010) with three mental retardation organizations, 350 employees (direct caregivers, house leaders, and staff members) contracted and licensed by the State of Tennessee, the study concluded that transformational leadership was the dominant leadership style in mental retardation organizations, while laissez-faire leadership style was the least. Transactional leadership also exists in mental retardation organizations. The study also found a significant difference in leadership styles among mental retardation organization administrators, and there is a strong correlation with caregivers' job satisfaction and transformational leadership.

Military Industry

As noted in a job satisfaction study conducted with 190 military/government employees and support contractors by Bell-Roundtree (2004), employees reported increase job satisfaction and commitment attitudes to the organization when leaders displayed the five transformational leadership behaviors. "These attitudes are associated with knowledge-worker retention, intrinsic motivation, improved customer relations and improved performance, as well as with decreased incidences of burnout and counterproductive behaviors" (p. 109). This research also "establishes a positive relationship among universal job satisfaction and organizational commitment" (p. 109).

In a job satisfaction study conducted with active duty women who served in the Air Force, in the healthcare profession, during Operation Iraqi Freedom and Operating Enduring Freedom (operations in Afghanistan). Blankenship (2010), noted "the study served to extend the body of research that suggest behaviors of leaders, especially those that display transformational and transactional leadership behaviors with a higher degree of frequency, as perceived by their subordinates" (p. 5). Such behaviors elicit an advanced level of job satisfaction and obligation. However, the findings were inclusive that leadership behavior "had as strong of a relationship as an individual's commitment to their profession or the job within itself" (p. 5).

Education Industry

Chu (1993) used a qualitative study to define the level of job satisfaction of 629 full-time schoolteachers from a private vocational system. The author concluded that the overall transformational leadership and subscales were definitely associated with general job satisfaction. The female teachers perceived their principals had more leaders that are transformational and less laissez-faire leaders than the male teachers.

Nicholson (2003) conducted a job satisfaction study of 114 teachers from 331 schools. The research indicated a direct, negative relationship between the principal's transactional leadership style and student's achievement. The study also noted that there were no significant relationships found between student achievement and the transformational leadership and the teacher's job satisfaction variables.

In another job satisfaction study conducted by Kirkman (2004) in a community college, where data were collected from seven department chairs and 22 supervised faculties, this study did not confirm, and even implied a possible reversal, of the notion that transformational leadership led to greater job satisfaction. The relationship determined between leadership style and effectiveness of department chairs in a community college setting and faculty job satisfaction were an anomaly in this situation when contrasted to previous studies for other types of institutions. The faculty job satisfaction in this instance did not increased because the department chairs practicing more transformational leadership style in the community college.

In a job satisfaction study conducted with 51 students from Walden University by Handsome (2009), the study determined that job satisfaction increased with leaders who possessed transformational leadership style, and decreased with leaders who possessed laissez-faire leadership style. Handsome also noted that there was strong evidence of a statistically significant, moderately strong positive correlation between job satisfaction and the transformational leadership style. The study conducted by Handsome donated to social change by recognizing the type of leadership styles, which provided support to job satisfaction and assist the organization to create strategies to improve job satisfaction, which could increase workers retention, quality, and income (Handsome, 2009).

In a job satisfaction study conducted with 131 full-time and part-time/adjunct faculty members who taught at three community colleges in Southern, CA. Abou Harash (2010), the findings suggested that faculty members who work for a transformational leader had a greater level of job satisfaction than those who worked for a transactional leader, with the exception of transformational leaders, who scored high on the transactional subscale of Contingent Rewards. Faculty members with an undergraduate degree were more satisfied overall than the faculty with a terminal degree. The study also noted that there were no significant differences between full-time and part-time faculty in regards to job satisfaction.

Gaps in the Research

Because of the review of the literature for this study, the majority of the employees perceived their leaders to possess and display a transformational or transactional style and less of a laissez-faire style (Gates, 2009; Handsome, 2009). In most of the studies presented, subordinates were more receptive of the transformational and transactional leadership styles, and there was a positive association among the employee's satisfaction and organizational commitment (Bell-Roundtree, 2004; Lin, 2003; Kirkman 2004). Some studies found no significant correlation among the perceived style of the leader and the level of job satisfaction of the subordinate (Lange, 2008; Wood, 2010).

Of the twenty different studies noted in the current study literature review, few of the studies conducted involving city and state leaders and employees, seven studies were from the medical industry, and two studies were from the military. One study was from the music industries, four studies were from the manufacturing industry, and there are five studies noted from the academia or community college environment. Base on the researcher's review, there were no studies that dealt with employee's (or departmental staff members) perceived leadership style of the leader nor how the leadership style impact the employee's level of job satisfaction within the community college environment. With this in mind, community colleges environment need more studies conducted, and more specifically, colleges located within the North Texas region of the United States.

Conclusion

A review of the literature indicates additional research is required to explore whether relationships existed between the employee's perception of the leader's style of leadership and how the leader's style impact the employee's level of job satisfaction. Previous research showed correlation does exist in most studies found and reported by the researcher; however, the literature review did not address the relationships between the employee's perception of the leader's style of leadership and the employee's job performance. The use of different industries could be more indicative of the general population because the sampling is from a broader group.

Summary

The literature review of the current study help fill space of the existing research. The research design should result as insight into the phenomenon of job satisfaction through the exploration of the correlation between the leader's style of leadership and the employee's level of job satisfaction within one of the North Texas community college districts (Creswell, 2005). Chapter 3 introduces the research methods used for the current study.

Chapter 2 included the current study's literature review, both historical and current findings, which exist in the fields of leadership style and job satisfaction. The focus of the literature review in Chapter 2 included eleven areas: title searches, articles, research documents, journal research, research question, literature review, styles of leadership, community colleges, MLQ-5x relevant studies, MSQ relevant studies, and the gaps discovered relating to the current study. The literature research revealed to the researcher that there was no studies found directly relating to the departmental employee's job satisfaction at the collegiate level. The majority of the education related studies founded focused on the job satisfaction of the administrators and faculty (Abou Harash, 2010; Chu, 1993; Handsome, 2009; Kirkman, 2004, Nicholson, 2003).

Chapter 3 will include the review of the current study's research methodology. The focus of the current study's research methodology includes twelve areas: research method, design appropriateness, population, sampling, informed consent, confidentiality, geographic location, data collection, instrumentations, internal validity, external validity, and the data analysis of the selected research methodology as they relates to this study regarding leadership styles and job satisfaction in the workplace within a community college environment.

Chapter 3

Research Methods

The purpose of this quantitative study was to measure the relationship between the subordinate's perceived leadership style of the leader and level of the subordinate's level of job satisfaction. Chapter 3 includes the review of the current study's research methodology and the explanation of the data collection process. The focus of the current study's research methods in Chapter 3 includes twelve areas: research method, design appropriateness, population, sampling, informed consent, confidentiality, geographic location, data collection, instrumentations, internal validity, external validity, and data analysis of the selected research methodology as they relates to this study regarding leadership styles and job satisfaction in the workplace within a community college environment.

Research Method and Design Appropriateness

The current study involves the use of a quantitative method to collect and analyze data received from the sample population regarding a leader's style of leadership perceived by the subordinates and how the subordinates rates their level of satisfaction with their job. According to Creswell (2005), when conducting a quantitative study, the researcher must identifies the research questions, identify or create an instrument to gather the data when the questions are answered, and analyze the data using figures, data, and facts. The current study will collect and analyze data regarding the subordinate's level of job satisfaction from the instructional and support departments located throughout the seven community college campuses (Brookhaven College, Cedar Valley College, Eastfield College, El Centro College, Mountain View College, North Lake College, and Richland College) located in Dallas, Texas.

The quantitative method ensures the current study is specific and narrow, whereby the researcher can uncover measurable, observable data on the variables. Quantitative research enables the research to collect data from instruments with preset questions and responses, and acquire data from a large population (Creswell, 2005). The participants in the current study from the instructional departments included individuals with the following job titles: academic vice presidents, academic deans, academic program coordinators, faculty, academic administrative assistants, and academic instructional associates. The support department personnel include individuals with the following job titles: student services/support vice presidents, student services/support deans, student services/support administrative assistants, and student services/support staff members and other non-instructional personnel.

The surveys were distributed to the sample population by accessing a SurveyMonkey© website link through the Dallas County Community College District's (DCCCD) e-mail system (Microsoft Outlook) for the researcher to collect the results of the sample population's perception of perceived leadership and level of job satisfaction. Using the DCCCD's e-mail system allowed the researcher to ensure only individuals in the sampling process would represent the target population. The purpose of a survey was to collect information from the sample population and develop the figures that create the quantitative descriptions of the collected data (Salkind, 2006). According to Creswell (2005), researchers have increasingly used e-mail and websites to collect survey data.

The Multifactor Leadership Questionnaire Form 5X Short, 3rd ed. (MLQ-5x) (see Appendix E), developed by Burns (1995) and refined by Avolio and Bass (2004), was used to define the leader's style of leadership. The Minnesota Satisfaction Questionnaire Short Form, 1977 (MSQ) (see

Appendix G), developed by Weiss, Dawis, England, and Lofquist (1977) was used to measure the job satisfaction of the instructional and support department employees. A demographic survey (see Appendix D) was used to cover to questions pertaining to subordinates, such as sex, age, ethnicity, education level, job title, length of employment, employment status, and department. The data collected enabled the researcher to respond to the research question and testing of each hypothesis. An analysis of the collected data were required to conclude if there is a relationship between the subordinate's perceived leadership styles of the leader and the level of the subordinates' job satisfaction of the instructional and support departments' personnel within a North Texas community college environment.

Population

The sample population in the current study consisted of 292 employees working in the seven local community colleges of the Dallas County Community College District (DCCCD) (Brookhaven College, Cedar Valley College, Eastfield College, El Centro College, Mountain View College, North Lake College, and Richland College) located in North Texas. The population consisted of full-time and part-time employees from the instructional and support departments. The target population in the current study consisted of approximately 7,300 full-time and part-time employees. The population in the current study consisted of subordinates employed by the DCCCD during the 2013-2014 academic year.

Sampling

The sample in the current study covers subordinates in the instructional and support departments from among the seven campuses (Brookhaven College, Cedar Valley College, Eastfield College, El Centro College, Mountain View College, North Lake College, and Richland College) within the Dallas County Community College District (DCCCD). The current study consisted of three independent variables (transformational, transactional, and laissez-faire) and one dependent variable (job satisfaction: "very satisfied," "satisfied," "neither satisfied nor dissatisfied," "dissatisfied," and "very dissatisfied"). The researcher used the G*Power Data Analysis software to calculate the power analysis for the current study (Faul, Erdfelder, Buchner, & Lang, 2009). The researcher plans to use the *t tests* as the test family, *means* [difference between two dependent means (matched pairs)], and a *priori* power analysis (used to compute required sample size – given α, power, and effect size). The input parameters includes the following: the level of statistical significance (alpha) equals *.05*, the power criterion equals *.95*, and the effect size equals *.30* to calculate the number of participants needed for the current study (Creswell, 2005). The output parameters includes the following: the Noncentrality parameter σ equals *3.64*, the Critical t equals *2.62*, the degree of freedom equals *146*, the total sample size equals *147*, and the actual power equals *.95* (See Figure 2).

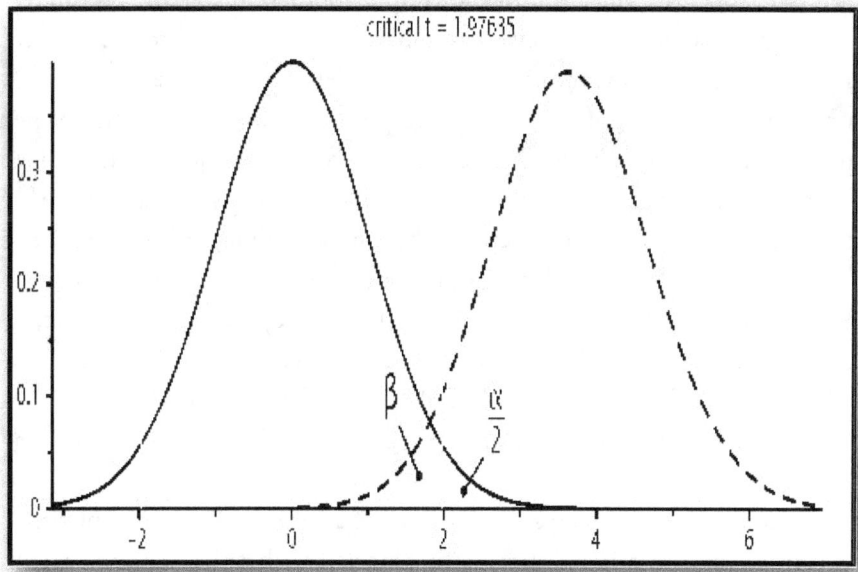

Fig 2. G*Power Analysis Results (Introduction to SAS.
UCLA: Statistical Consulting Group)

The current study plans to count all data received from the sample population as two experimental groups (instructional and support department).

An e-mail was sent out district-wide by the researcher to notify the potential subordinates who wish to participate within the current study. The researcher anticipated surveying personnel from within the Dallas county region. The surveyed individuals represented a variety of ethnic, cultural traditions and diverse values.

Informed Consent

The Chancellor of the Dallas County Community College District (DCCCD) approved a premise, recruitment, and name use form to authorize the researcher to distribute the surveys to the sample population (see Appendix A). In addition, the DCCCD's IRB Board approved the current research proposal, which included faculty representation from all seven campuses (see Appendix B). Prior to the sample population starting the surveys, the potential participants received an e-mail with one attachment: an introductory e-mail (see Appendix B) specifying details about the nature of the current study, risks, confidentiality of responses, and the time commitment required for each participant. Participants proceeded to complete the surveys once they verify their age (18 and older) and agreed to participate in the current study. Every participant received the same e-mail regarding the purpose of the current study. The demographic survey was confidential. Once the surveys were completed and recorded by the SurveyMonkey© website, the results was collected by the researcher and exported into the IBM Statistical Package for the Social Sciences (SPSS) v22 database. The researcher compiled the data of the raw scores and properly secured all information for additional analysis.

While taking the surveys, a participant had the choice of completing or not completing the surveys after getting started with either survey. The invitation e-mail informed the participants how to withdraw from the study without penalty. The researcher did not used the surveys with incomplete data from participants who decide to opt out of the data collection or during the analysis of the current research. The current study did not include face-to-face interviews.

Confidentiality

For the sake of maintaining privacy of the participants and the protection of human subjects and confidentially, the survey results did not include the names of the participants or used any identifying information for data analysis. Each survey automatically received a number or code to identify each individual survey forms completed by each individual participant. The results of the data collected might be used in future publications and presentations, while ensuring the privacy of the participants. All survey data were aggregate formatted. To protect the participant's privacy, the researcher will not publish none of the individual survey responses and data.

The survey data from the current study is located on the researcher's laptop hard-drive and an external back-up drive and both maintained in the researcher's possession. The current study information was accessible with a unique password only known and assigned by the researcher. The researcher did not know which participant submitted which response. The researcher will destroy the research data after three years after publication. The researcher will delete current research data all research files on the researcher's laptop to the "recycle bin". Afterward, the researcher will permanently delete all of the current research data by using a DISKKeeper or similar program to delete the data.

Geographic Location

The research for the current study focused on selected employees employed by the seven community colleges (Brookhaven College, Cedar Valley College, Eastfield College, El Centro College, Mountain View College, North Lake College, and Richland College) of the Dallas County Community College District (DCCCD) located in Dallas, Texas. The population consisted of full-time and part-time employees from the instructional and support departments of the selected community college campuses. The target population in the current study consisted of approximately 7,300 employees in the instructional and support departments located across the selected community college campuses. If fewer than 147 individuals completed the surveys, the researcher had planned to hold forums on each campus in order to generate enough interest from the selected population to participate and complete the current study. Forums were not necessary, due to the fact; the researcher received 293 responses during the initial time set aside to collect the data. The researcher did not use coercion or gimmicks in order persuade the participation in the current study. Participants in the current study volunteered to participate in the current study. The researcher had association with the community colleges selected for the research. To maximize the recruitment of participants, an e-mail was sent out via the DCCCD's e-mailing system to each community college to announce the survey to the potential participants and provided the SurveyMonkey© website link for those who wished to participate in the current study.

Data Collection

This current study used one method or technique to collect the data. The survey method of collecting data were conducted by each participant using the SurveyMonkey© website to collect the data for this study. The sample participants had a total of18 day to complete the surveys. Once the data were collected and downloaded, the researcher generated a Likert-scale type result spreadsheets/database of the three survey instruments [demographic surveys (see Appendix D), MLQ Form 5x – Short (see Appendix E), and the MSQ Short Form (see Appendix G)] to analyze the collected data from each participant. None of the surveys required personally identifying information. The researcher instructed participants to avoid placing their name, return address, or any identifying information on the surveys to guarantee anonymity. In most studies, the conclusion of the study required data that are not tainted or distorted. For this reason, the researcher maintained strict control over all data collected by not sharing the responses from any participants.

The rationale for the researcher using this type of technique for the current study was because a Likert scale/database was generally used and common in survey research. Likert scales recognized as summated-rating or additive scales because the scores are generated by adding the number of responses provided (Neuman, 2003). The data collected from the MLQ-5x and MSQ instruments required a scoring system. Scoring required the researcher to assign numeric score to each response category for each question (Creswell, 2005). The current study generated descriptive statistics. Descriptive statistics identify trends, variance, range, and standard deviation for the data collected for a variable (Creswell, 2005). The quality and the collection of the data must be consistent. Each participant had equal time and opportunity to respond to all questions without any undue pressure or persuasion.

In addition to informing the participants of the purpose of the current study, the instructions informed the participants that their participation would be voluntary. The participants consented upon the completion of the survey. If a participant did not complete a survey, the data from that particular survey was not included in the analysis. There were no face-to-face interviews conducted in the current study.

The kind of data collected by the researcher for the current study included the survey results collected from the sample population from the three survey instruments: (1) the Multifactor Leadership Questionnaire Form 5X Short, 3rd ed. (MLQ-5x) (see Appendix E), (2) the Minnesota Satisfaction Questionnaire Short Form, 1977 (MSQ) (see Appendix G), and (3) the demographic survey (see Appendix D).

The MLQ-5x survey data included forty-five descriptive statements (see Appendix E) of the employee's judgment of how frequently each statement fits their respective leader using the following rating scale:

Not at all	Once in a while	Sometimes	Fairly often	Frequently, if not always
0	1	2	3	4

The MSQ survey data included twenty descriptive statements (see Appendix G) to give the employee the chance to tell *how they feel about their present job*, what things they were *satisfied* with and what things they were *not satisfied* with.

Very Dissatisfied	Dissatisfied	Neither Satisfied nor Dissatisfied	Satisfied	Very Satisfied
		2	4	
1		3		5

Based on their answers and those of people like them, the researcher hoped to gain a better understanding of the things people *like and dislike about their jobs*. The employees chose from the following statement to describe *how satisfied they feel about the aspect of their job*:

* if you feel that your job gives you *more than you expected*, check the box under *"Very Sat."* (Very Satisfied);
* if you feel that your job gives you what *you expected*, check the box under *"Sat."* (Satisfied);
* if you *cannot make up your mind* whether or not the job gives you what you expected, check the box under *"N."* (Neither Satisfied nor Dissatisfied);
* if you feel that your job gives you *less than you expected*, check the box under *"Dissat."* (Dissatisfied);
* if you feel that your job gives you *much less than you expected*, check the box under *"Very Dissat."* (Very Dissatisfied);

The demographic survey data included the sample population responses to questions pertaining to the employees, such as sex, age, ethnicity, education level, job title, length of employment, employment status, and department (see Appendix D). The data collection process was appropriate for the research design and problem for the current study because the process needed to involve five interrelated steps: (1) select participants, (2) obtain permission, (3) decide what type or types of data to collect, (4) locate, modify, or develop instruments, and (5) actually collecting the data (Creswell, 2005). The data collected from the participants meeting the current study eligibility requirements was stored on the computer in the researcher's locked office for the duration of the study and for a period of 3 years after the study. The completed survey results will be stored in the IBM Statistical Package for the Social Sciences (SPSS) v22 database. The Excel file will be located on a password-protected computer, which will be stored in the office of the researcher. After completion of the data collection and entry of the data, the researcher conducted the data analysis by using the data analysis tools found in the IBM's SPSS software. Upon completion of the research, the data shall remain in a secured computer file for 3 years. The data will be scheduled for destruction by spring of 2017, at the end of the archival period by DISKKeeper, software that is used to destroy confidential data.

Instrumentation

In a quantitative study, the researcher uses an instrument to measure the variables from the study. Usually, the tool contains specific questions and response possibilities that were pre-established or developed in advance of the study. The participants and research location selected is intentional to best understand the core phenomenon being studied. On-line data collection tools are valuable and convenient. A well-constructed on-line study can potentially make use of data collection strategies and tactics that simply cannot be obtain by the use of paper and pencil (Jones, 2010). A demographic survey was developed (see Appendix D) to address questions pertaining to the employees, such as sex, age, ethnicity, education level, job title, length of employment, employment status, and department. The demographic survey took approximately 3 to 5 minutes to complete.

The MSQ survey instrument measured the subordinate's level of satisfaction with his or her job. The MSQ survey took approximately 15 minutes for each participant to complete. A sample copy of the survey questions for the MSQ survey instrument (Appendix G) consisted of 20 questions. The MSQ short form consists of 20 facets (See Table 3.1).

Table 3.1

Facets from the Minnesota Satisfaction Questionnaire (MSQ)

Activity
Ability application
Accomplishment
Accountability
Appreciation
Change
Colleagues
Company policies and practice
Control (technical)
Creativeness
Individuality
Management (human relations)
Moral values
Payment
Power
Progress
Refuge
Social service
Social status
Working Situations

Source: Weiss, Dawis, England, and Lofquist (1967).

As a leading research tool, the MLQ-5x survey instrument is associated with leadership. The MLQ-5x was reported as one of the most widely used instruments to measure the leader's behavior in the organizational sciences and the instrument which assist the subordinates to learn how they perceived the leader's style of leadership with whom they work (Sahaya, 2012; Vrba, 2007; Zopiatis & Constani, 2012). The MLQ-5x survey took approximately 30 minutes to complete. The MLQ-5x Survey consisted of 45 questions. A sample copy of the survey questions for the MLQ-5x survey instrument found in Appendix E.

The MLQ-5x, as shown in Table 3.2, is the instrument that measures transformational leadership, transactional leadership, and laissez-faire leadership (Eagly, Johannesen-Schmidt, & van Engen, 2003).

Table 3.2

Definitions of Scales, Subscales, and Description of Leadership Styles (MLQ–5x)

MLQ–5x scales with subscales	Description of Leadership Style
Transformational	
Idealized Influence (attribute)	Identified by one having reverence and self-importance by association with others
Idealized Influence (behavior)	Identified by one knowing and believing in the core values and mission of the workplace
Inspirational Motivation	Identified by one being positive and showing enthusiasm toward the goals and direct of the workplace
Intellectual Stimulation	Identified by one searching for difference ways of resolving issues and accomplishing the mission
Individualized Consideration	Identified by one concerned about coaching, mentoring, and helping others
Transactional	with their needs
Contingent Reward	Identified by one awarding acceptable performance
Management by Exception (active)	Identified by one focusing on the shortcomings of others
Management by Exception (passive)	Identified by one who is hesitant to intervene
Laissez-faire	Identified by one who is usually absence and hate to get involve during the most serious times

Source: MLQ-5x = Multifactor Leadership Questionnaire – Form 5x

Reliability

The reliability of the MLQ-5x (see Appendix E) was based on a number of validity studies, including the relationship of the instrument with the five-factor model of personality. In a study conducted by Kanste, Miettunen, and Kynga (2007), the MLQ-5x was noted as a reliable instrument for internal consistency and stability. "The MLQ-5x's subscales ranged between 0.78 and 0.94. The inter-item correlations ranged between 0.30 and 0.70. The coefficient values at two measurements points ranged between 0.77 and 0.86. The MLQ-5x instrument can be used in academic leadership education" (p. 206). The MLQ-5x instrument was used to "determine if academic program leaders in college used transformational, transactional, or laissez-faire leadership styles in performing their duties" (Jones & Rudd, 2008, p. 88). At three Malaysian Universities, a study determined the dean's leadership style and its correlation with leadership usefulness (Sadeghi & Pihie, 2012). In Carter's (2009) study, MLQ-5x's ranged from .74 to .94 reliabilities for each items and the leadership factor scale. According to Shibru and Darshan (2011), who used the MLQ-5x instrument to evaluate the influences of transformational, transactional, and laissez-faire leadership, "the instrument has excellent validity and reliability (as cited in Lievens, Geit & Coetsier, 1997) which was confirmed by researchers and used extensively throughout the world" (p. 290). For this study, "seventeen subject matter experts analyzed the questionnaire and included those fulfilled the requirement based on Lawshe (1975) content validity ratio measurement scale (CVR)" (Shibru & Darshan, 2011, p. 290).

The MSQ (see Appendix G) instrument had an underlying rationale. The instrument was based on empirical research, provide reliable scores and it have evidence of construct validity. Evaluations of construct validity for the MSQ were based on confirmation of predictions from theory (Weiss, Dawis, England, & Lofquist, 1967). According to Buitendach and Rothmann (2009), the MSQ is reliable and the instrument confirmed the two-factor structure during the investigation of job satisfaction of selected employees. The test-retest reliabilities ranged between 0.70 and 0.80 with an alpha coefficient of 0.5. As noted by Yin-Fah, Yeoh, Lim, and Osman (2010), the MSQ is a popular measurement to conceptualize job satisfaction. During a study conducted by Wang, Tolson, Chiang, and Huang (2010) noted the MSQ as being a reliable instrument to measure intrinsic satisfaction, extrinsic, and general satisfaction. The MSQ instrument was tested or calculated in three different ways: Coefficient α, item analysis, and factor analysis. The Coefficient α was consistent high, ranging between .82 and .93. The item analysis showed that each item had a positive correlation, ranging between .36 and .72. The factor analysis emerges two factors: the percentage of variance associated with the first factor ranged between 83.2 and 92.6 and the eigenvalue associated with the second factor never exceeded 1.0 (Wang, Tolson, Chiang, & Huang, 2010, p. 152).

Validity

The validity of a test is what the test is intended to do (Salkind, 2006). Salkind noted that there are three aspects of validity when a test instrument is used:

1) Validity refers to the test outcome and not the test.
2) The results of the test are not just acceptable or unacceptable. This progress occurs in degrees whether or not there is low validity or high validity.
3) The validity of the results interprets in how the test occurs.

According to Neuman (2003), validity refers to the degrees to which a study provides truthful results and the degree to which the concepts and measures fit together. The validity and reliability of the results depend on two factors: (a) the validity and reliability of the survey instrument and (b) the extent to which the results of the data analysis meet the criteria for the reliability of the chi-square test of independence. Several measures of validity are possible, such as face, criterion, concurrent, construct, convergent, and discriminant. External validity refers to the extent to which one may generalize the study findings. Internal validity refers to the extent to which one may have confidence that the explanation of the dependent variable is acceptable as the correct explanation.

A number of observations regarding the validity of the study are appropriate. Face validity for the survey instrument exists to the extent that the aspects of organizational culture identified and the questions on organizational culture types reflect generally accepted views regarding these topics (Harrison & Stokes, 1992). Concurrent, convergent, and discriminant forms of validity for the survey instrument exist to the extent that the survey structure and method are very similar to that of Cameron and Quinn's (1999) survey instrument.

Internal Validity

As noted by Creswell (2005), internal validity is consider as a problem that threatens the researcher's ability to draw a conclusion based on his or her experiences or the experiences of the participants. The current study design is to discover the valid conclusions about the correlations between the dependent variable, job satisfaction, and the independent variables, transformational, transactional, and laissez-faire leadership styles.

The internal consistency and test-retest were the criteria used to assess the reliability. Instruments with an internal consistency coefficient of .80 were adequate. The test-retest coefficient of .70 was adequate. In a study conducted by Carless (1998), "MLQ-5x (Avolio et al., 1995) was used to assess transformational leadership. The three subscales of charisma (referred to as attributed charismatic leadership; 8 items, alpha = .91), individualized consideration (9 items, alpha = .93), and intellectual stimulation (10 items, alpha = .92), were employed" (p. 353). In a study noted by üstüner (2009), the MSQ internal consistency of the scale was ".96", and the test-retest correlation was ".88." The Pearson correlation coefficient examines test-retest reliability between sets of scores to demonstrate the stability of the scores (Creswell, 2005). Coefficients that range from .20 to .35 indicate a slight relationship, coefficients that fall within the range of .35 to .65 are useful for limited prediction, coefficients that fall within the range of .66 to .85 are good for predictions, and coefficients of .86 and above are the desired reliability of researchers for test-retest and construct validity. Neuman (2003) noted that there are no errors internal to the design of the research project.

External Validity

Neuman (2003) noted that external validity was necessary to generalize findings from a particular situation and small group to a more comprehensive setting and large group. The current study will consist of a small controlled population sample, which may reduce the threat to external validity. Ensuring the external validity of the current study, the convenience sample of the instructional and support employees participating in the research included employed part-time and full-time in the community college environment.

The external validity of a research study is the "extent to which conclusions drawn can be generalized to other contexts". Creswell (2005) discussed three types of validity: content validity, criterion-related validity, and construct validity (p. 165). Content validity measures how well the questions represent the possibilities of questions available. Criterion-related validity measures how well the scores on the instrument relate to the outcome. Construct validity measures what the scores on the instrument signify (Creswell, 2005).

Data Analysis

The researcher received and retained the responses from each survey instrument (MLQ-5x, MSQ, and demographic) from the SurveyMonkey© website and maintained the results in an IBM Statistical Package for the Social Sciences (SPSS) v22 database file. After receiving the data, the researcher assigned numeric scores or values to the data for each response category, for each question collected, on each survey instruments. The researcher sorted and analyzed the collected data in an aggregate format.

The IBM (SPSS) data analysis tool selected by the researcher was suitable for the current study to explain the variations between the dependent and independent variables (Neuman, 2003). The researcher used the Pearson's correlation coefficient (rho) to show how much two variables "go together" or covary (Neuman, 2003). Descriptive statistics described the trends in the data for each of the variables (means, standard deviation, and sample sizes) (Creswell, 2005).

The data analyses technique selection was appropriate for the current study research design because the technique allow for statistical testing of the data received from each survey instruments. Statistical testing was used to test the null and alternative hypotheses to conclude if a statistically significant correlation exists between the subordinate's perceived leadership style (transactional, transformational, and laissez-faire) of the leader and the level of the subordinate's job satisfaction (very satisfied, satisfied, neither satisfied nor dissatisfied, dissatisfied, or very dissatisfied). The researcher tested the hypotheses by using a two-tailed test with a 5% alpha level. The statistical significance was set at the .95 level (Creswell, 2005).

To display the compared statistical findings of the sample population of the current study in an aggregate format, the researcher identifies the various themes and introduces the information in tables, figures, and graphs (Creswell, 2005). Finally, the researcher created a narrative of the current study by restating the research question and stating the discovery applicable to the question, which will help support the framework of the researcher's interpretation. In addition, the researcher reviewed and compared similar literature, note the observed limitations, and made appropriate recommendations for future studies because of the current study.

Summary

Chapter 3 explained the methodology used in the current study. Specific information about the population was provided, as well as, how the data were collected electronically from the SurveyMonkey© website. Other researchers and empirical documentation validated each instrument (Kim, 2009). In addition, the researcher provided the identification and process steps of the data analysis.

In Chapter 3, the researcher provided an outline of the research methodology, a justification for the design's appropriateness, population information, sampling number, review of data collection, selection of the survey instrument, validity of the current study. In addition, the researcher provided the identification of data analysis of the current study regarding leadership styles and job satisfaction in the workplace within a community college environment (Creswell, 2005).

Chapter 4 includes a report of the distinct outcomes related to the research process of the current study, and description of statistical procedures. Expository and figures will be used to describe the data and test the hypotheses. Chapter 4 also includes a report of the consequences and an explanation of the findings created by the data analysis. The data will be presented by using a variety of difference tables (Creswell, 2005).

The focus of the current study's results in Chapter 4 includes eight areas as they relate to the current study regarding leadership styles and job satisfaction in the workplace within a North Texas community college environment: purpose of the study, population, sample selection, data collection, demographics, research questions, reliability testing, and hypotheses testing (Creswell, 2005).

Chapter 4

Results

The intent of this quantitative study was to measure the relationship between the subordinate's perceived leadership style of the leader and the subordinate's level of job satisfaction. The general problem was to assist the leader in identifying their type of leadership style; how their subordinates perceived their style of leadership; and how their style of leadership related to the level of their subordinate's job satisfaction. The specific problem investigated perceived leadership style of the leader by the subordinate and how the subordinate's perception of the leadership style determines the level of job satisfaction of the subordinates in the workplace in a community college environment.

The 262 voluntarily participants completed the MLQ-5x survey (see Appendix E), MSQ survey (see Appendix G), and a demographic survey (see Appendix D). The MLQ-5x survey was used to measure perceived the leadership style (transformational, transactional, and laissez–faire - independent variables) of the leaders and the MSQ survey was used to measure the level of job satisfaction (dependent variable) of the subordinates within one of the North Texas community college district subordinates. Participants in the current study completed a demographic questionnaire.

In Chapter 4, the researcher discusses the methodology, research questions, hypotheses, process of collecting data, and the analysis of the data. Also, the researcher provides the results of the demographics, how the employees perceives their leader's style of leadership, and the degree of the subordinates' job satisfaction, and the comparison of the survey data between the two sample groups: instructional and support departments. In addition, a concluding summary of the findings completes this chapter.

Research Question and Hypotheses

Research Question
One research question was formulated for this study, RQ1: What is the relationship between the subordinate's perceived style of leadership of the leader and the subordinate's level of job satisfaction within the instructional and support departments within one of the North Texas community college districts? Correlations between the perceived leadership style of the leader (MLQ-5x) (see Appendix E) and the levels of job satisfaction (MSQ) (see Appendix G) were identified for each department to answer the research question.

Hypotheses
Through an examination of relationships, the researcher identified the levels of job satisfaction for each group and the relationships between the variables were determined. The analysis included testing the following hypotheses:

$H1_0$: There is no relationship between the subordinate's perceptions of the leader's style (the degree to which a leader uses) of transformational leadership and the subordinate's job satisfaction level within the instructional and support departments in one of the North Texas community college districts.

$H1_a$: There is a positive relationship between the subordinate's perceptions of the leader's style (the degree to which a leader uses) of transformational leadership and the subordinate's job satisfaction level within the instructional and support departments in one of the North Texas community college districts.

$H2_0$: There is no relationship between the subordinate's perceptions of the leader's style (the degree to which a leader uses) of transactional leadership and the subordinate's job satisfaction level within the instructional and support departments in one of the North Texas community college districts.

$H2_a$: There is a positive relationship between the subordinate's perceptions of the leader's style (the degree to which a leader uses) of transactional leadership and the subordinate's job satisfaction level within the instructional and support departments in one of the North Texas community college districts.

$H3_0$: There is no relationship between the subordinate's perceptions of the leader's style (the degree to which a leader uses) of laissez–faire leadership and the subordinate's job satisfaction level within the instructional and support departments in one of the North Texas community college districts.

$H3_a$: There is a negative relationship between the subordinate's perceptions of the leader's style (the degree to which a leader uses) of laissez–faire leadership and the subordinate's job satisfaction level within the instructional and support departments in one of the North Texas community college districts.

Research Instruments

The Multifactor Leadership Questionnaire (MLQ) Form 5x-Short

For the MLQ-5x (see Appendix E) (Bass & Avolio, 2004) instrument, the participants replied to each question by selecting one of the five responses: *not at all, once in a while, sometimes, fairly often, and frequently, if not always.* The responses were coded by the researcher using a scale of 0 to 4, with 0 representing *not at all*, 1 representing *once in a while*, 2 representing *sometimes*, 3 representing *fairly often*, and 4 representing *frequently, if not always* and the results were entered into a data table. The three leadership styles (independent variables - transformational, transactional, and laissez-faire) and their subscales are measured by the MLQ-5x instrument. The first style is transformational leadership with five subscales. The second style is transactional leadership with two subscales. The third style is laissez-faire (passive/ avoidant) leadership with two subscales. The Table 4.1 addressed the three leadership styles and the subscales that makes up each leadership style. The outcomes of leadership in the current study has three subscales (Avolio & Bass, 2004). Subscales 1–5 measure transformational leadership, subscales 6–7 measure transactional leadership, and subscales 8–9 measure passive/ avoidant leadership styles.

Table 4.1

Leadership Styles and Subscales (MLQ-5x)

Leadership Styles	Subscales
Transformational	Ideal influence (Attributes) (IA)
	Ideal influence (Behaviors) (IB)
	Inspirational motivation (IM)
	Intellectual stimulation (IS)
	Individualized consideration (IC)
Transactional	Contingent reward (CR)
	Management by exception: Active (MA)
Passive/Avoidant	Management by exception – Passive (MP)
	Laissez-faire (LF)
Outcomes of Leadership	Extra Effort (EE)
	Effectiveness (EF)
	Satisfaction (SA)

The MLQ-5x instrument was also designed to measure the outcomes of leadership which determine how the subordinate perceives his or her leader as a motivator and informs how satisfied the subordinate is with how the leader work with others. Subscales 10–12 measure outcomes of leadership. In addition, the MLQ-5x instrument helps determine leader's outcome of leadership: *Extra Effort, Effectiveness, and Satisfaction.* The scoring method for the MLQ-5x instrument is found in Table 4.2 (Avolio & Bass, 2004).

Table 4.2

Subscales of Leadership Styles, Item Numbers, and Scoring Method (MLQ-5x)

Subscales for Leadership Styles	Items Number	Scoring Method
Ideal influence (Attributes) (IA)	10, 18, 21, 25	Sum of items divided by 4
Ideal influence (Behaviors) (IB)	6, 14, 23, 34	Sum of items divided by 4
Inspirational motivation (IM)	9, 13, 26, 36	Sum of items divided by 4
Intellectual stimulation (IS)	2, 8, 30, 32	Sum of items divided by 4
Individualized consideration (IC)	15, 19, 29, 31	Sum of items divided by 4
Contingent reward (CR)	1, 11, 16, 35	Sum of items divided by 4
Management by exception – Active (MBEA)	4, 22, 24, 27	Sum of items divided by 4
Management by exception – Passive (MBEP)	3, 12, 17, 20	Sum of items divided by 4
Laissez-faire (LF)	5, 7, 28, 33	Sum of items divided by 4
Outcomes of Leadership	Items that measure the outcomes of leadership	
Extra Effort (EE)	39, 42, 44	Sum of items divided by 3
Effectiveness (EFF)	37, 40, 43, 45	Sum of items divided by 4
Satisfaction (SAT)	38, 41	Sum of items divided by 2

The Minnesota Satisfaction Questionnaire (MSQ) Form

For the MSQ (see Appendix G) (Weiss, Dawis, England, & Lofquist, 1967) instrument, the participant responded to each question by selecting one of the five responses: *very dissatisfied, dissatisfied, neither, satisfied, or very satisfied*. Responses were coded by the researcher using a scale of 1 to 5, with 1 representing *very dissatisfied*, 2 representing *dissatisfied*, 3 representing *neither dissatisfied nor satisfied*, 4 representing *satisfied*, and 5 representing *very satisfied*, and the results were entered into a data table.

The MSQ measured the level of job satisfaction. The subordinate's level of job satisfaction is the dependent variable. The components of the dependent variable consist of : a) *intrinsic* - job satisfaction which is dependent on the individual's perception and internal feeling and includes factors such as recognition, advancement, and responsibility, b) *extrinsic* - external job related variable which include the individual's salary, supervision, and working conditions, and c) *overall satisfaction* – the combination of both intrinsic and extrinsic. The following tables (see Table 4.3 and Table 4.4) specify the types of job satisfaction, their subscales, item numbers, and the scoring methods (Avolio & Bass, 2004).

Table 4.3

Type of Job Satisfaction and Subscales Definition (MSQ)

Type of Job Satisfaction	Subscales of Each Type
Intrinsic (I)	Intrinsic means internal or inside of you.
Extrinsic (E)	Extrinsic means external or outside of you.
Overall Satisfaction (O)	All subscales added together

Table 4.4

Subscales of Job Satisfaction, Items Numbers, and Scoring Method (MSQ)

Type of Job Satisfaction	Items Number	Scoring Method
Intrinsic (I)	1, 2, 3, 4, 7, 8, 9, 10, 11, 15, 16, 20	Sum of items divided by 12
Extrinsic (E)	5, 6, 12, 13, 14, 19	Sum of items divided by 6
Omit	17 and 18 (Not included in Intrinsic or Extrinsic)	
Overall Satisfaction (O)	Sum of 1 – 20 added together	Sum of items divided by 20

Dependent and Independent Variables

The study consisted of the leader's style of leadership as the independent variables (*transformational, transactional,* and *laissez-faire*). The MLQ-5x survey instrument measured the independent variables. The independent variables dictate the style of leadership displayed by the subordinates' leader, supervisor, or manager. The current study also identified and examined the correlation of the sample population (employees) between two different departments as independent variables: instructional and support. The employees who work within the instructional department usually work in an instructional division (i.e.: Business and Technology, Math and Science, or Liberal Arts), which provides administrative assistance directly to the deans, coordinators, faculty, other instructional staff members, and students. The employees who work within the support department usually work in a support division (Information Technology Help Desk, Business Office, Student Services, or Facility), which provides support and operational assistance directly to the instructional divisions, president's office, Marketing Department, and other support areas across the campus. The current study consisted of *job satisfaction* as the dependent variable (intrinsic, extrinsic, and overall satisfaction). The MSQ survey instrument measured the dependent variable. The dependent variable describes the types of satisfaction exhibited by the subordinates. The intrinsic component of job satisfaction includes the employee's perception and feelings when one receives acknowledgement, promotion, and responsibility. The extrinsic component of job satisfaction includes the employee's perception and feeling when one receives higher income, better supervision, and improved working environment.

Description of the Population

The sample group for the current study consisted of instructional departments' employees (academic vice presidents, academic deans, academic program coordinators, faculty, academic administrative assistants, and academic instructional associates. The support departments' employees (student services/support vice presidents, student services/support deans, student services/support administrative assistants, student services/support staff members and other non-instructional employees) from the seven community college campuses (Brookhaven College, Cedar Valley College, Eastfield College, El Centro College, Mountain View College, North Lake College, and Richland College) within the Dallas County Community College District (DCCCD).

Demographics

A demographic survey was developed to obtain the subordinate employees' sex, age, ethnicity, education level, job title, length of employment, employment status, and department (see Appendix D). Out of 7,300 employees in the DCCCD, 292 employees responded by either completing or partially completing the surveys. The general response rate for this study was 4.0%. A total of 29 surveys were declared unusable out of 292, which reduced the response rate to 3.60%. Of the 263 completed surveys, 157 (59.6%) were completed by employees who worked in an instructional department. A total of 106 (40.3%) employees who worked in a support department completed the surveys. Overall, across the DCCCD, 48 (18.2%) full-time administrators completed the surveys, 62 (23.5%) full-time faculty completed the surveys, 38 (14.4%) part-time faculty completed the surveys, and 45 (17.1%) full-time professional support staff completed the surveys (see Table 4.5).

Table 4.5

Employment Status of the Survey Participants by Departments

Instructional Department	n	%	Support Department	n	%
Administrator Full-time	25	15.9	Administrator Full-time	23	21.7
Faculty Full-time	60	38.2	Faculty Full-time	2	1.9
Faculty Part-time	33	21.0	Faculty Part-time	5	4.7
Profession Support Staff Full-time	33	21.0	Profession Support Staff Full-time	12	11.3
Professional Support Staff Part-time	6	3.8	Professional Support Staff Part-time	64	60.4
Total	157	100 %	Total	106	100%

The ages of the participants ranged between 18 to 60+ years. 19.2% were between 39 and 45 years of age, 16.1% were between 46 and 52 years of age, 24.1% were between 53 and 59 years of age, and 23.0% were 60+ years of age. Of the 262 respondents, 34.7% were Black/African American, 9.2% were Hispanic American, and 52.3% were White Caucasian.

Data Collection

During the month of February 2014, the data for this study were collected from the MLQ-5x (see Appendix E) (Bass & Avolio, 2004) and MSQ (see Appendix G) (Weiss, Dawis, England, & Lofquist, 1967) instruments. The MLQ-5x was used to identify the subordinates' perceived style of leadership by the leaders. The MSQ was used to determine the subordinates' level of job satisfaction of the employees who were employed by the Dallas County Community College District (DCCCD) during the academic school year of 2013-2014. The researcher sent out an introductory e-mail (see Appendix C), through the DCCCD's e-mail system called Microsoft 2013 Outlook, to the District personnel, which included individuals from the seven community college campuses (Brookhaven College, Cedar Valley College, Eastfield College, El Centro College, Mountain View College, North Lake College, and Richland College) where the instructional and support department employees worked.

Each respondent received an e-mail which included the SurveyMonkey© link embedded in the e-mail. When the participant read the e-mail and agreed to take the surveys, the e-mail directed the participant to click on the link provided to access the surveys. If the participant refused to participate, the researcher omitted the respondent from the study. Approximately, 7,300 potential participants received the introductory e-mail. 59.6% of the sample population was from the instruction department and 40.3% were from the support department. A total of 29 participants did not complete either part or all of one or more surveys. The surveys were available for 18 days for the DCCCD employees to give individuals enough time to participate by completing the surveys and for the study to have sufficient responses received to reach the 95% confidence level. Due to the positive responses (high number of participants of 263 employees) during the original time that the survey link was available, no additional solicitation was required to reach the minimal number of participants of 134 as presented in Chapter 3.

Data Analysis

Demographic Analysis

After collecting the data, the researcher used the IBM Statistical Package for the Social Sciences (SPSS) v22 data analysis software to analyze the data and generate reports. The demographic survey included information relating to the gender, years of employment of working in the DCCCD, employment status, and the educational level of the participants (see Table 4.5, Table 4.6, Table 4.7, Table 4.8 and Table 4.9). In the instructional department, the full-time and part-time faculty members had two times the number of participants in the study then the number of administrators and professional support staff (PSS) combined. Of the 263 respondents, 40.3% were from the support department. In the support department, the data showed that three times the number of professional support staff (PSS) participated in the study than the number of administrators and faculty members (see Table 4.5)

In the instructional department, the number of female participants outnumbered the male participants 2:1. The employees who were 60+ years of age consisted of 30.3% of the workforce and the White/Caucasian and Black/African American made up over 88.4% in the instruction department (see Table 4.6).

Table 4.6

Descriptive Statistics for Gender, Age Group, and Ethnicity for the Instructional Department

Demographics		n	%
Gender			
Male		49	31.2
Female		108	68.8
	Total	157	100.0
Age Group			
18 – 24		1	0.6
25 – 31		6	3.9
32 – 38		12	7.7
39 – 45		27	17.4
46 – 52		28	18.1
53 – 59		34	21.9
60+		47	30.3
	Total	155	100.0
Ethnicity			
American Indian or Alaskan Native		5	3.2
Asian / Pacific Islander		5	3.2
Black or African American		47	30.1
Hispanic American		8	5.1
White / Caucasian		91	58.3
	Total	156	100.0

In the support department, the number of female participants also outnumbered the male participants 2:1. The employees who were 39 – 60+ years of age made up of over 74.6% of the workforce and the White/Caucasian and Black/African American made up over 84.9% of the workforce in the support department (see Table 4.7).

Table 4.7

Descriptive Statistics for Gender, Age Group, and Ethnicity of the Support Department

Demographics		n	%
Gender			
Male		34	32.1
Female		72	67.9
	Total	106	100.0
Age Group			
18 – 24		2	1.9
25 – 31		13	12.3
32 – 38		12	11.3
39 – 45		23	21.7
46 – 52		14	13.2
53 – 59		29	27.4
60+		13	12.3
	Total	106	100.0
Ethnicity			
American Indian or Alaskan Native		0	0.0
Asian / Pacific Islander		0	0.0
Black or African American		44	41.5
Hispanic American		16	15.1
White / Caucasian		46	43.4
	Total	106	100.0

In the instructional department, individuals with a master and doctorate degree consisted of 78% of the total participants. The employees employed from 17 years or less made up 75% of the workforce (see Table 4.8).

Table 4.8

Descriptive Statistics for Education Level and Time Worked for the Instructional Department

Demographics		n	%
Education Level			
GED		0	0.0
HS Diploma		4	2.6
Associate Degree		11	7.1
Bachelor Degree		18	12.2
Master Degree		86	55.1
Doctorate Degree		36	23.1
	Total	155	100.0
Time Worked in the DCCCD			
0 – 2 yrs.		22	14.2
3 – 5 yrs.		18	11.6
6 – 8 yrs.		19	12.3
9 – 11 yrs.		23	14.8
12 – 14 yrs.		17	11.0
15 – 17 yrs.		17	11.0
18 – 19 yrs.		5	3.2
20 – 21 yrs.		4	2.6
22 – 24 yrs.		5	3.2
25 – 27 yrs.		3	1.9
28 – 30 yrs.		1	0.6
30+ yrs.		21	13.5
	Total	155	100.0

In the support department, individuals with a bachelor and master degree consisted of 74% of the total participants. The employees who were employed 14 years or less made up 82% of the workforce (see Table 4.9).

Table 4.9

Descriptive Statistics for Education Level and Time Worked for the Support Department

Demographics		n	%
Education Level			
GED		1	0.9
HS Diploma		6	5.6
Associate Degree		12	11.2
Bachelor Degree		33	30.9
Master Degree		48	44.9
Doctorate Degree		7	6.5
	Total	107	100.0
Time Worked in the DCCCD			
0 – 2 yrs.		27	25.2
3 – 5 yrs.		27	25.2
6 – 8 yrs.		8	7.5
9 – 11 yrs.		12	11.2
12 – 14 yrs.		14	13.2
15 – 17 yrs.		4	3.7
18 – 19 yrs.		1	0.9
20 – 21 yrs.		2	1.9
22 – 24 yrs.		4	3.7
25 – 27 yrs.		6	5.6
28 – 30 yrs.		1	0.9
30+ yrs.		1	0.9
	Total	107	100.0

Descriptive Analysis

Descriptive analysis defined the central tendency and variability of the sample data. The researcher used the mean, mode and median in the study to describe the central tendency and standard deviation to define the variability. A correlation test was used to determine if there was a relationship between the subordinate's perceived style of leadership of the supervisors of the participants in this study as measured by the MLQ-5x and the subordinate's level of job satisfaction measured by the MSQ (see Appendix I).

First, the correlations indicated that transformational leadership style was positively correlated with the overall job satisfaction ($r(261) = .720$, $p<.001$), intrinsic job satisfaction subscale ($r(261) = .637$, $p<.001$), and extrinsic job satisfaction subscale ($r(261) = .775$, $p<.001$) (see Appendix I). As transformational style of leadership increases the employee's overall job satisfaction, intrinsic job satisfaction subscale, and extrinsic job satisfaction subscale increase.

Second, the correlations indicated that laissez-faire leadership style was negatively correlated with the overall job satisfaction ($r(261) = -.650$, $p<.001$), intrinsic job satisfaction subscale ($r(261) = -.557$, $p<.001$), extrinsic job satisfaction subscale ($r(261) = -.697$, $p<.001$), and transformational leadership style ($r(261) = -.766$, $p<.001$) (see Appendix I). As laissez-faire style of leadership increases the employee's overall job satisfaction, intrinsic job satisfaction subscale and extrinsic job satisfaction subscale decrease.

Third, the correlations indicated that extra effort subscale outcome of leadership was positively correlated with the effectiveness subscale outcome of leadership ($r(261) = .829$, $p<.001$) (see Appendix I). As extra effort subscale outcome of leadership increases the effectiveness subscale outcome of leadership increases.

Forth, the correlations indicated that the satisfaction subscale outcome of leadership was positively correlated with both the extra effort subscale outcome of leadership ($r(261) = .830$, $p<.001$) and effectiveness subscale outcome of leadership ($r(261) = .899$, $p<.001$) (see Appendix I). As the satisfaction subscale outcome of leadership increased, the extra effort subscale outcome of leadership and the effectiveness subscale outcome of leadership increase.

A *t-test* (see Table 4.10) tested for group differences (Instructional and Support Departments) (Creswell, 2005). The IBM Statistical Package for the

Social Sciences (SPSS) v22 software analyzed the data while evaluating each hypothesis at the *alpha* of .05 (α) level of significance.

Table 4.10

Compare the T-test Results between the Leadership Styles and the Overall Job Satisfaction between the Instructional and Support Departments

Measure	Department	n	M	SD	t	df
Overall Satisfaction (O)	Instructional	157	3.8	0.67	1.28*	205
	Support	106	3.7	0.76		
Transformational (TF)	Instructional	157	2.5	0.96	0.15*	213
	Support	106	2.4	1.02		
Transactional (TA)	Instructional	157	2.0	0.64	0.57*	231
	Support	106	2.0	0.60		
Laissez-faire (LF)	Instructional	157	1.2	0.95	0.78*	225
	Support	106	1.1	0.94		

Note. * = P > 0.05

A paired-samples t-test was conducted to determine the significant different of the leaders' perceived leadership styles in both departments (independent variables) and the significant different of the overall job satisfaction (dependent variable) in both departments. There is no significant difference of the overall job satisfaction between the instructional department (M=3.8; SD=0.67) and the support department (M=3.7; SD=0.76). However, there is significant difference of the transformational leadership style between the instructional department (M=2.5; SD=0.96) and the support department (M=2.4; SD=1.02) (See Table 4.10).

In addition, when comparing the overall job satisfaction measure with the three styles of leadership (transactional, transformational, and laissez-faire), the current study revealed that the transactional leadership style has a greater amount of degree of freedom (*df* = 231) (See Table 4.10). Greater the chance, more accurately the entire population is sampled. The degree of freedom varied because data derived from two-sample unequal variances (instructional and support departments). Although the number of observations were consisted, the responses for each survey question by each participant may not be constant.

The researcher used multiple regression analysis to exam the relationship between the perceived styles of leadership dimension and job satisfaction dimension. As represented in Table 4.11, there was a direct conclusion of the analysts that significantly explained 63% of the variability in job satisfaction. The result indicated that transformational leadership style was unrelated to extrinsic job satisfaction within both the instructional department (B=0.50, p>0.05) and within the support department (B=0.58, p>0.05). Laissez-faire leadership style was statistically significant, however had a weak relationship with extrinsic job satisfaction within the instructional department (B=-0.23, p<0.05) and within the support department (B=-0.29, p<0.05).

Table 4.11

Regression Analysis of Transformational, Transactional, and Laissez-faire Styles of Leadership and Job Satisfaction between the Instructional and Support Departments (n=264)

Dimensions	Department	Intrinsic Job Satisfaction	Extrinsic Job Satisfaction	Overall Job Satisfaction
Transformational	Instructional	0.41*	0.50*	0.43*
	Support	0.38*	0.58*	0.41*
Transactional	Instructional	-0.07	0.03	-0.04
	Support	-0.28	-0.12	-0.25
Laissez-faire	Instructional	-0.08	-0.23	-0.14
	Support	-0.23	-0.29	-0.27
R^2	Instructional	0.43	0.63	0.56
	Support	0.46	0.63	0.56
AdjR^2	Instructional	0.42	0.63	0.55
	Support	0.44	0.62	0.54
F Value	Instructional	38.4	88.7	65.6
	Support	28.5	57.8	42.7

* Correlation is significant at the 0.05 level (2 tailed)

Hypotheses Analysis

Hypothesis #1 Finding:
Based on the results of the current study, there is a positive relationship between the transformation leadership style and the overall job satisfaction. Based on the results of the correlation data in Appendix I, the transformational style of leadership showed statistically significant ($r(263) = .721$, $p<.001$). The null hypothesis was rejected.

Hypothesis #2 Finding:
Based on the results of the current study, there is a positive relationship between the transactional leadership style and the overall job satisfaction. Based on the results of the correlation data in Appendix I, the transactional style of leadership showed less significant ($r(263) = .366$, $p<.001$). The null hypothesis was rejected.

Hypothesis #3 Finding:
Based on the results of the current study, there is a negative relationship between the laissez–faire leadership style and the overall job satisfaction. Based on the results of the correlation data in Appendix I, the laissez-faire style of leadership had a negative relationship with job satisfaction ($r(263) = -.650$, $p<.001$). The null hypothesis was rejected.

Findings

Demographic Analysis
The demographics of the sample population who participated in the current research study included 263 employees with 180 (68%) females and 83 (32%) males. Employees in the instructional departments tend to capitalize on their

tenure around 15 – 17 years, while the employees in the support departments tend to work in the departments until the age of the late 50's. Education beyond an associate degree was significant in both departments. Employees in the instructional departments obtained more doctorate degrees, while 90% of the sample population had an associate degree or higher.

Descriptive Analysis.
Descriptive analysis provided the results of central tendency and variability of the survey answers received from the sample population. From the perception of the leaders' style of leadership, transformational and transactional leadership (MLQ-5x) occurred within the workplace of where the employees worked at the seven colleges based on the mean responses of *fairly often* (3 points), and *frequently, if not always* (4 points). Overall, the transformational leadership styles mean score was higher than the transactional mean score. The research study measured job satisfaction (MSQ) from its subscales and an overall approach. The subscales approach measured satisfaction of the subordinates of *intrinsic* and *extrinsic*. The study showed the employees responded more or preferred intrinsic job satisfaction to extrinsic job satisfaction.

Conclusion
The research study assessed the relationship of the subordinates' perception of their leaders and the impact on their job satisfaction within the instructional and support departments in one of the community college districts located in North Texas. The current study examined how his or her subordinates perceive the supervisor's leadership behavior and how it relates to the subordinate's job satisfaction. The researcher concluded that the leadership behavior styles were beneficial in order to promote positive or significant job satisfaction of community college employees in the instructional and support departments.

Summary

In Chapter 4, the researcher presented the descriptive statistics and the related analyses of the data collected for the study. Chapter 4 included how the researcher collected the data and selected difference methods used to analyze the data. The research question and the hypotheses restated in Chapter 4, which supports theoretical background of the current study. The researcher discussed the collection of the data, characteristics of the population samples, and the different survey instruments used in the study.

The results of the analyses rejected all three null hypotheses and determined that there was sufficient evidence to conclude that the perceived leadership style of the leader can influence the level of job satisfaction among employees within the instructional and support departments in a community college environment. The findings show that the subordinates' perceived transformational and transactional leadership styles of their leader plays a large role in the impact on their level of job satisfaction in the workplace.

The results and findings aligned with the research questions and hypotheses in Chapter 4. Chapter 5 explains the analyses of the data presented in Chapter 4, which include the significant research questions, hypotheses, conclusions, and the results. In addition, Chapter 5 will provide the findings, implications, conclusions, and recommendations for future research.

Chapter 5

Conclusion and Recommendations

The purpose of this quantitative study was to measure the relationship between the subordinate's perceived leadership style of the leader and the subordinate's level of job satisfaction. The research question for this study focused on the perceived leadership style of the leader and the level of job satisfaction of the subordinates within the instructional and support departments in one of the North Texas community college districts. The transformational, transactional, and laissez-faire styles of leadership and the two department groups were the independent variables. The dependent variables were the levels of job satisfaction.

The two types of academic work groups were instructional and support department employees. This study identified the subordinates' level of job satisfaction for each work group. Correlations between the perceived leadership style of the leader (MLQ-5x) (see Appendix E) and the levels of job satisfaction (MSQ) (see Appendix G) were identified for each department. The results of the study answered the following research question: What was the relationship between the subordinate's perceived style of leadership of the leader and the subordinate's level of job satisfaction within the instructional and support departments of one of the North Texas community college districts? The researcher conducted the current study to help academic leaders know and understand how their subordinates perceived their style of leadership and how the perception of their leadership style influences the subordinates' level of job satisfaction.

Chapter 5 provides the conclusion for the current study. In addition, Chapter 5 includes recommendations for the current study, which investigated the perceived leadership style of the leader and the level of job satisfaction of the subordinate within the instructional and support departments in one of the North Texas community college districts. In this chapter, the researcher includes the findings and interpretations, compare findings, and suggestions for future research. A summary of the study completes the chapter.

Findings and Interpretations

The findings in this study may be useful for the sustainability and growth of an academic institution. The senior administrators and other leaders at various levels throughout the institution and different departments should be reminded how their subordinates perceived their styles of leadership and how the subordinate's perception influences the level of job satisfaction of their employees (Jernigan & Beggs, 2005; Amah, 2009). When the leaders of the institution do not address the perception of their subordinates and the subordinates' level of job satisfaction, the results could have a negative impact on the primary stakeholder, which is the student's persistent, graduation rates, and student success.

The negative impact could lead to employee burnout, absenteeism, frustration, and hinder the overall mission and sustainability of the education institution (Amah, 2009; Ram & Prabhakar, 2010). The impact of poor leadership and low job satisfaction leads to low creativity; customer service; enthusiasm; morale; organizational commitment; productivity; and self-valued (Mor Barak, Travis, Pyum, & Xie, 2009). Poor leadership is demonstrated when leaders do not perform the *right* (ethical) action(s) for his or her organization, co-workers, staff, and subordinates. Toxic leadership behavior of the leader can and will interfere with the attitude, moral, physical and mental well-being, and performance of others within the organization (Mehta & Maheshwari, 2013).

The results of this study can be applicable to any higher education institution or major corporation. The current study could assist administration and management to understand the importance of providing training to their leadership team members regarding their style of leadership and the increase job satisfaction among their employees. The results of this study may contribute more emphasis on the academia leaders in the Dallas County Community College District, who is determined to increase their intrinsic and extrinsic leadership skills to promote positive student behavior, increase subordinates level of job satisfaction, and create and transform aspiring leaders.

The finding of the current study was similar to the studies in Chapter 2, because each researcher identified in the literature review used the MLQ-5x and MSQ instruments to conduct his or her appropriate study. Most of the studies were similar, because each study identified or stated that the laissez-faire style of leadership was more likely to cause dissatisfaction upon the employees (Bass, 1990). Transformational style of leadership was noted as having a greater significant in each study then the transactional or laissez-faire leadership styles of leadership.

The finding of the current study were different than the other studies included in Chapter 2, because the researcher review several studies in five different industries, such as education, manufacturing, military, music, and medical. The current study was different because the researcher focused on the leaders in the community college environment in only two departments: instructional and support. The current study was different from the other studies, because the researcher used the study to obtain the opinion of the subordinates about their leaders and shed some light on the importance of the roles played by the subordinates within the organization (Avolio, 2011).

In comparison to other studies found in Chapter 2, one of the strengths of the current study include the ability of the researcher to survey individuals within a local college district, located in North Texas. The current study focused on the instructional and support departments and did not include other workgroups. An additional strength of the current study included the fact the researcher current held the position of an executive division dean.

A weakness of the current study included the researcher did not consider or examine the different facets of job satisfaction (pay, promotion, and co-workers) and their impact on job satisfaction (DeRue & Ashford, 2010; Hasan & Subhani, 2011). Another weakness regarding the current study, the researcher did not include other colleges in the North Texas area to participate in the current study. Another weakness of the current study, the research did not include more details and examples about the results or the consequences of how having a dissatisfied employee and his or her impact on the organization. The above-mentioned weaknesses could have negatively influenced the current study, causing the study to have too board of a focus. However, the researcher may use these weaknesses in future studies to explore job satisfaction from a different perspective.

Research Question and Hypotheses

Research Question

The researcher formulated one research question for this study, which focused on the perceived leadership styles of the leader and the level of job satisfaction of the subordinates within the instructional and support departments in a community college environment. Correlations between the perceived leadership style of the leader (MLQ-5x) (see Appendix E) and the levels of job satisfaction (MSQ) (see Appendix G) identified for each departments to answer the research question:

RQ1: What is the relationship between the subordinate's perceived style of leadership for the leader and the subordinate's level of job satisfaction within the instructional and support departments in one of the North Texas community college districts?

Hypotheses

Positive or negative relationships, the levels of job satisfaction of each group were identified and the relationships between the variables were determined. The analysis included testing the following hypotheses:

$H1_0$: There is no relationship between the subordinate's perceptions of the leader's style (the degree to which a leader uses) of transformational leadership and the subordinate's job satisfaction level within the instructional and support departments in one of the North Texas community college districts.

$H1_a$: There is a positive relationship between the subordinate's perceptions of the leader's style (the degree to which a leader uses) of transformational leadership and the subordinate's job satisfaction level within the instructional and support departments in one of the North Texas community college districts.

Hypothesis 1 investigated the relationship between the subordinate's perceptions of the leader's style (the degree to which a leader uses) of transformational leadership and the subordinate's job satisfaction level within the instructional and support departments in one of the North Texas community college districts. The analysis showed a positive and significant relationship existed between the job satisfaction (intrinsic and extrinsic) and the transformational leadership behavior styles of idealized influence, inspirational motivation, intellectual stimulation, individualized consideration, and contingent reward.

$H2_0$: There is no relationship between the subordinate's perceptions of the leader's style (the degree to which a leader uses) of transactional leadership and the subordinate's job satisfaction level within the instructional and support departments in one of the North Texas community college districts.

$H2_a$: There is a positive relationship between the subordinate's perceptions of the leader's style (the degree to which a leader uses) of transactional leadership and the subordinate's job satisfaction level within the instructional and support departments in one of the North Texas community college districts.

Hypothesis 2 explored the relationship between the subordinate's perceptions of the leader's style (the degree to which a leader uses) of transactional leadership and the subordinate's job satisfaction level within the instructional and support departments in one of the North Texas community college districts. The transactional leadership analysis showed a more positive and significant relationship existed between the job satisfaction (intrinsic and extrinsic). The transactional leadership behavior style was more desired than that of the transformational leadership behavior, which was identified in previous research noted in Chapter 2.

H3$_0$: There is no relationship between the subordinate's perceptions of the leader's style (the degree to which a leader uses) of laissez–faire leadership and the subordinate's job satisfaction level within the instructional and support departments in one of the North Texas community college districts.

H3$_a$: There is a negative relationship between the subordinate's perceptions of the leader's style (the degree to which a leader uses) of laissez–faire leadership and the subordinate's job satisfaction level within the instructional and support departments in one of the North Texas community college districts.

Hypothesis 3 explored the relationship between the subordinate's perceptions of the leader's style (the degree to which a leader uses) of laissez–faire leadership and the subordinate's job satisfaction level within the instructional and support departments in one of the North Texas community college districts. The laissez-faire leadership behavior was the least desired by the employees in the current study. Most employees are more productive under leaders who are goal driven and those who understand and know value of strong leadership.

Suggestions for Future Research

The researcher provided six recommendations for consideration in regards the relationship between subordinate's perceived leadership style of the leader and level of the subordinate's job satisfaction are provided: First recommendation is to repeat the research utilizing a large sample population. Second recommendation is to repeat the study of the relationship between the leadership members of each department or management group and the leader's direct reports or subordinates. Third recommendation is to examine the differences between the community college's and university's instructional and support departments in respect to comparing the subordinate's perceived leadership style of the leader and level of the subordinate's job satisfaction.

Fourth recommendation is to examine the perceived leadership style of the leader and level of the subordinate's job satisfaction between different size college, type of institution (private or state), and geography location compared to like colleges. Fifth recommendation is to duplicate the research with socio-economic, represented ethnic and cultural groups. Sixth recommendation is have future studies to examine the leadership styles of specific leaders in higher education, such as academic vice presidents of instruction, executive deans of all divisions, or faculty coordinators from specific disciplines. Seventh recommendation is for the future studies to include college districts, located in North Texas. Eighth recommendation is for future studies to include the different facets of job satisfaction (pay, promotion, and co-workers) and their impact on job satisfaction in the college districts, located in North Texas. Ninth recommendation is for the future studies to provide more details and examples about the results or the consequences of how having dissatisfied employees and what their impact may have on the organization. Although this study had a small sample size, a larger sample size may not change the results, but may have help strengthen the findings and the conclusions.

Summary and Conclusion

The community college requires highly qualified individuals with demonstrated skills and ability to serve its primary customer (the student) and support their internal and external customers, while handling multiple tasks in order to help the institution reach its goals and objectives. The workplace environment in the community college requires order, quality, strong leadership, and satisfied employees are productive and successful over a long period.

Leaders throughout the organization must know how to lead his or her department in order to create and maintain a substantive level of productivity. Leaders need the help of his or her subordinates to create, build, and maintain a customer-centered organization. Most subordinates tend to lose focus when they are not valued or satisfied on their job.

Leaders should remember that the style of the leader's leadership influences the employee job satisfaction, sets the tone in the office, and inspires the completion of assigned tasks. The organization is able to achieve and maintain great customer service due to having a high level of employee job satisfaction. Leaders influence how their subordinates and coworkers respond to each other, handle the pressure of day-to-day activities, and increase their desire as an intrigue part of the organization. The organization leadership recognizes job satisfaction in workplace happens when employees are happy and they feel motivated. Job satisfaction is depended upon the employee's response in the workplace to physical psychological, social, and cognitive stimuli.

This quantitative research study evaluated the relationships of perceived leadership styles of the leader to the subordinates' job satisfaction in several community colleges located in the North Texas area. Chapter 5 concluded the evaluation of the relationships by arriving at four conclusions: (1) relationships does exist between the perceived leadership behavior styles of the leader and the job satisfaction of his or her subordinates; (2) transformational leadership predicted a high level of job satisfaction among college employees; (3) transactional leadership predicted a high level of job satisfaction among college employees; and (4) laissez-faire leadership style was less desired by employees who wanted to have a high level of job satisfaction.

The operational implications of this study requires leaders to know and understand the impact of their employees' perception of their style of leadership and the impact on the job satisfaction and productivity of their employees. Also, the administration should remember that the failure of leaders knowing and understanding the outcomes of this study may lead to unsatisfied employees, high absenteeism, high turnover, chaotic or hostile work environment, and the failure to meet and exceed the organization goals. To help prevent these things from transpiring, a leader may attend professional development training sessions, which focus on leadership styles, emotional intelligence, and personality traits and he or she must have the time to implement the new tools and concepts learned from such training.

References

Abou Harash, H. (2010). *An analysis of the relationship between the perceived leadership styles of educational leaders and the job satisfaction of faculty members who serve under them with community colleges* (Doctoral Dissertation). Available from ProQuest Dissertations and Theses database. (UMI No. 3423555)

Abualrub, R. F. & Alghandi, M. G. (2012). The impact of leadership styles on nurses' satisfaction and intention to stay among Saudi nurses. *Journal of Nursing Management, 20*(5), 668-678. Retrieved April 2, 2014 from EBSCOhost database.

Adebayo, O. O. (2010). *Obstetric nurses' perceptions of manager's leadership style on job satisfaction and organizational commitment* (Doctoral Dissertation). Available from ProQuest Dissertations and Theses database. (UMI No. 3468112)

Adekola, B. (2012). Work Burnout Experience among university non teaching staff: A gender approach. *International Journal of Academic Research in Business & Social Sciences, 2(1)*, 128-135. Retrieved February 28, 2013from ProQuest database.

Allio, R. (2013). Leaders and leadership – many theories, but what advice is reliable? *Strategy & Leadership, 41*(1), 4-14. Retrieved February 28, 2013from ProQuest database.

Altaf, A. & Awan, M. A. (2011). Moderating affect of workplace spiritually on the relationship of job overload and job satisfaction. *Journal of Business*

Ethics, 104(1), 93-99. Retrieved December 27, 2011 from EBSCOhost database.

Altundemir, M. E. (2012). The impact of the financial crisis on American public universities. *International Journal of Business and Social Science, 3*(8). Retrieved December 26, 2012 from ProQuest database.

Amah, O. E. (2009). Job satisfaction and Turnover Intention Relationship: The moderating effect of job role centrality and life satisfaction. *Research and Practice in Human Resource Management, 17*(1), 24-25. Retrieved July 20, 2013 from EBSCOhost database.

American Association of Community Colleges (2012). *About Community Colleges.* Washington, DC: American Association of Community Colleges. Author.

Anonymous (2009). Strong leadership vital to firms' futures, warns Jones. *The Safety & Health Practitioner, 27*(8), 28. Retrieved April 3, 2014 from ProQuest database.

Ansari, N. G. (2011). Employee perception of HRM practices: Impact on commitment to the organization. *South Asian Journal of Management, 18*(3), 122-149. Retrieved March 1, 2013 from ProQuest database.

Arcidiacono, C., Procentese, F., & Di Napoli, I. (2009). Qualitative and quantitative research: An ecological approach. *International Journal of Multiple Research Approaches, 3*(2), 163-176. Retrieved July 20, 2013 from EBSCOhost database.

Arms, D. (2012). Effective learning and development programs are crucial. *Strategic Finance, 93*(8), 8-10. Retrieved April 16, 2012 from EBSCOhost database.

Ashley, B. (2008), The ABCs of strong leadership. *Air & Space Power Journal, 22*(2). Retrieved April 3, 2014 from ProQuest database.

Avolio, B. J. (2011). *Full range leadership development.* Thousand Oaks, CA: Sage.

Avolio, B. J. & Bass, B. M. (2004). Multifactor Leadership Questionnaire, Third Edition. *Mental Measurements Yearbook, 17.* Retrieved January 29, 2012 from EBSCOhost database.

Avolio, B. J., Bass, B. M., & Jung, D. I. (1999). Re-examining the components of transformational and transactional leadership using the Multifactor Leadership Questionnaire. *Journal of Occupational & Organizational Psychology, 72*(4), 441-62. Retrieved January 1, 2012 from EBSCOhost database.

Ayers, D. F. (2010). Putting the community back into the college. *Academe, 96*(3), 9-11.
Retrieved January 5, 2013 from EBSCOhost database.

Azorin, J. M. & Cameron, R. (2010). The application of mixed methods in organizational research: A literature review. The *Electronic Journal of Business Research Methods, 8*(2), 95- 105. Retrieved May 30, 2011 from EBSCOhost database.

Bakotic, D. & Babic, T. (2013). Relationship between working conditions and job satisfaction: The case of Croatian Shipbuilding Company. *International Journal of Business and Social Science, 4*(2). Retrieved April 3, 2014 from ProQuest database.

Bambacas, M. & Patrickson, M. (2008). Interpersonal communication skills that enhance organizational commitment. *Journal of Communication Management, 12*(1), 51-72. Retrieved January 1, 2013 from ProQuest database.

Barrick, M. R. & Zimmerman, R. D. (2009). Hiring for retention and performance. *Human Resource Management, 48*(2), 183-206. Retrieved December 28, 2011 from EBSCOhost database.

Basham, M. J., Stader, D. L., & Bishop, H. N. (2009). How "pathetic" is your hiring process? An application of the Lessig "pathetic dot" model to education hiring practices. *Community College Journal of Research and Practice, 33*(3/4), 363- 385. Retrieved December 28, 2011 from EBSCOhost database.

Bass, B. M. (1990). *Bass & Stogdill's handbook of leadership: Theory, research, and managerial applications (3ʳᵈ ed.).* New York: Free Press.

Bass, B. M. & Avolio, B. J. (2004). *Multifactor Leadership Questionnaire (3ʳᵈ ed.).* Palo Alto, CA: Mindgarden.

Bell-Roundtree, C. V. (2004). *Does manager behavior influence knowledge worker job satisfaction and organizational commitment attitudes? A validation of Kouzes and Posner's transformational leadership theory* (Doctoral Dissertation). Available from ProQuest Dissertations and Theses database. (UMI No. 3119012)

Bennis, W. (1991). Creative Leadership. *Leadership Excellence, 8*(8), 5. Retrieved January 1, 2012 from EBSCOhost database.

Bennett, T. M. (2009). A study of the management leadership style preferred by its subordinates. *Journal of Organizational Culture, Communication and Conflict, 13*(2), 1-25. Retrieved January 1, 2012 from EBSCOhost database.

Blankenship, S. L. (2010). *The consequences of transformational leadership or transactional leadership in relationship to job satisfaction and organizational commitment for active duty women serving in the Air Force Medical Service* (Doctoral Dissertation). Available from ProQuest Dissertations and Theses database. (UMI No. 3398823)

Bloomdahl, S. C. & Navan, J. (2013). Student leadership in a residential college: From dysfunction to effective collaboration. *Journal of College Student Development, 54*(1), 110-114. Retrieved April 3, 2014 from ProQuest database.

Bolman, L. G. & Deal, T. E. (2003). Reframing Organizations: Artistry, Choice, and Leadership (3rd ed.). San Francisco: Jossey-Bass.

Brookmire, D. (2007). The time value of improved performance: Dealing with executives who have fatal flaws. *Human Resource Planning, 30*(2), 5-7. Retrieved April 5, 2014 from EBSCOhost database.

Bucic, T., Robinson, L., & Ramburuth, P. (2010). Effects of leadership style on team learning. Journal of Workplace Learning, 22(4), 228-248. Retrieved April 3, 2014 from ProQuest database.

Buitendach, J. H. & Rothmann, S. (2009). The validation of the Minnesota Job Satisfaction Questionnaire in selected organizations in South Africa. *South African Journal of Human Resource Management, 7*(1), 1 – 8. Retrieved March 25, 2012 from EBSCOhost database.

Cameron, K. S., & Quinn, R. E. (1999). *Diagnosing and changing organizational culture: Based on the competing values framework.* New York: Addison-Wesley.

Carless, S. A. (1998). *Assessing the discriminant validity of transformational leader behavior as measured by the MLQ, 71,* 353-358. Retrieved June 29, 2013 from ProQuest database.

Carlos, N. & Luke, W. J. (2012). A case study framework for community college leaders.
Community College Journal of Research & Practices, 36(4), 310-316. Retrieved April 2, 2014 from EBSCOhost database.

Carter, J. C. (2009). Transformational leadership and pastoral leader effectiveness.
Pastoral Psychology, 59(3), 261 – 271. Retrieved March 25, 2012 from EBSCOhost database.

Chen, H. (2005). *The influence of nursing director's leadership styles on Taiwanese Nursing faculty job satisfaction* (Doctoral Dissertation). Available from ProQuest Dissertations and Theses database. (UMI No. 3172100)

Chesney, D. L. (2012). Statistical judgments are influenced by the implied likelihood that samples represent the same population. *Memory & Cognition, 40*(3), 420-433. Retrieved January 1, 2012 from EBSCOhost database.

Cheung, M. F. Y. & Wong, C. (2011). Transformational leadership, leader support, and employee creativity. *Leadership & Organization Development Journal, 32*(7), 656-672. Retrieved April 3, 2014 from ProQuest database.

Childers, W., Adams, J. D., Jaffe, D., & Briskin, A. (2009). Transformational leadership and its relationship to trust and behavioral integrity. *Saybrook Graduate School and Research Center.* Retrieved January 1, 2012 from EBSCOhost database.

Chitwood, J. (2010). *Leadership style, employee satisfaction, and productivity in the enrollment department of a proprietary university* (Doctoral Dissertation). Available from ProQuest Dissertations and Theses database. (UMI No. 3471690) Christopher, M. & Matviuk, S. (2010). Impact of leadership on identifying right organizational designs for turbulent times. *IUP Journal of Soft Skills,* *4*(1/2), 57-67. Retrieved April 2, 2014 from EBSCOhost database.

Chu, I. Y. (1993). *The relationship of teachers' job satisfaction and their percep-tions of principals' leadership styles in private vocational high schools in a se-lected metropolitan area of Taiwan* (Doctoral Dissertation). Available from ProQuest Dissertations and Theses database. (UMI No. 9420287)

Chu, L. & Lai, C. (2011). A research on the influence of leadership style and job characteristics on job performance among accountants of county and city government in Taiwan. *Public Personnel Management,* *40*(2), 101-118. Retrieved May 30, 2011 from EBSCOhost database.

Ciftcioglu, A. (2011). Investigating occupational commitment and turnover in-tention relationship with burnout syndrome. *Business and Economics Research Journal,* *2*(3), 109-119. Retrieved January 1, 2013 from ProQuest database.

Cohrs, J. C., Abele, A., & Dette, D. E. (2006). Integrating situational and dis-positional determinants of job satisfaction: Findings from three samples of professionals. *Journal of Psychology,* *140*(4), 363-395. Retrieved January 3, 2012 from EBSCOhost database.

Cordeiro, W. P. (2010). A business school's unique hiring process. *Business Education Innovation Journal,* *2*(1), 56-60. Retrieved December 28, 2011 from EBSCOhost database.

Corey, M. S. & Corey, G. (2007). *Becoming a helper (5ᵗʰ ed.).* Mason, OH; Cengage Learning.

Creswell, J. W. (2005). *Educational Research: Planning, Conducting, and Evaluating Quantitative and Qualitative Research.* Upper Saddled River, NJ: Pearson Education, Inc.

Deluga, R. J. (1990). The effects of transformational, transactional, and lais-sez faire leadership, characteristics on subordinate influencing behavior. *Basic & Applied Social Psychology,* *11*(2), 191-203. Retrieved January 2, 2012 from EBSCOhost database.

Den Hartog, D. N., Van Muijen, J. J., & Koopman, P. L. (1997). Transactional versus transformational leadership: An analysis of the MLQ. *Journal of Occupational and Organizational Psychology,* *70*, 19-34. Retrieved January 1, 2013 from ProQuest database.

DeRue, D. S. & Ashford, S. J. (2010). Who will lead and who will follow? A social process of leadership identity construction in organizations. *Academy of Management Review, 35*(4), 627-647. Retrieved February 28, 2013 from EBSCOhost database.

Detamore, J. A. (2008). *An analysis of the relationships between job satisfaction, leadership, and intent to leave within an engineering consulting firm* (Doctoral Dissertation). Available from ProQuest Dissertations and Theses database. (UMI No. 3289494)

DuBrin, A. J. (1997). *Essentials of management (4th ed.).* Cincinnati, OH: South-Western College.

Dixon, G. (2009). Can we lead and follow? *Engineering Management Journal, 21*(1), 34
-41. Retrieved July 29, 2011 from EBSCOhost database.

Drew, G. M. (2010). Enabling or "real" power and influence in leadership. *Journal of Leadership Studies, 4*(1), 47-58. Retrieved April 16, 2012 from EBSCOhost database.

Eagly, A. H., Johannesen-Schmidt, M. C., & Van Engen, M. L. (2003). Transformational, transactional, and laissez-faire leadership styles: A meta-analysis comparing woman and men. *Psychological Bulletin, 129*(4), 569-591. Retrieved January 1, 2012 from EBSCOhost database.

Eichinger, B. (2007). Point: Is "build on your strengths" the best advice? *Human Resource Planning, 30*(4), 6 – 8. Retrieved April 21, 2008 from EBSCOhost database.

Ekaterini, G. (2010). The impacts of leadership styles on four variables of executives. *International Journal of Business and Management, 5*(6), 3-16. Retrieved May 30, 2011 from EBSCOhost database.

Ellis, P. & Abbott, J. (2013). Leadership and management skills in health care. *Nurse Prescribing, 11*(5), 251-254. Retrieved April 5, 2014 from EBSCOhost database.

Ezeabasili, S. (2010). *The interplay of leadership and job satisfaction in organization management of people with mental retardation* (Doctoral Dissertation). Available from ProQuest Dissertations and Theses database. (UMI No. 3418038)

Faul, F., Erdfelder, E., Buchner, A., & Lang, A.-G. (2009). Statistical power analyses using G*Power 3.1: Tests for correlation and regression analyses. *Behavior Research Methods, 41,* 1149-1160. Retrieved August 12, 2013 from http://www.psycho.uni-duesseldorf.de/abteilungen/aap/gpower3/.

Finn, M. L. (2008). *A quantitative study investigating relationships among leadership style, employee satisfaction and employee tenure* (Doctoral Dissertation). Available from ProQuest Dissertations and Theses database. (UMI No. 3324076)

Forde, A. V. (2011). *Job satisfaction and intention to quit among novice registered nurses: A quantitative correlational study* (Doctoral Dissertation). Available from ProQuest Dissertations and Theses database. (UMI No. 3514796)

Foster, D. E. (2002). A method of comparing follower satisfaction with the authoritarian, democratic, and laissez-faire styles of leadership. *Communication Teacher, 16*(2), 4-6. Retrieved April 5, 2014 from EBSCOhost database.

Freed, M. P. (2006). Learning to look forward. *Healthcare Financial Management, 60*(2), 138-144. Retrieved April 2, 2014 from EBSCOhost database.

Frick, D. (2011). Motivating the knowledge worker. *Defense AR Journal, 18*(4). Retrieved January 28, 2012 from ProQuest database.

Gates, S. M. (2009). *The relationship between supervisor leadership qualities and home-based clinician burnout* (Doctoral Dissertation). Available from ProQuest Dissertations and Theses database. (UMI No. 3357863)

Gentry, W. A., Katz, R. B., & Mcfeeters, B. B. (2009). The continual need for improvement to avoid derailment: A study of college and university administrators. *Higher Education Research & Development, 28*(3), 335-348. Retrieved May 24, 2009 from EBSCOhost database.

Gnage, M. F. & Drumm, K. E. (2010). Hiring for student success: A perspective for community college presidents. *New Directions for Community Colleges, 152,* 71-80. Retrieved April 2, 2014 from EBSCOhost database.

Goslin Jr., R. A. (2012). Driving toward effective leadership. *On Balance, 8*(3), 12-13.

Gregory-Mina, H. J. (2009). Technology in practice. *Leadership & Organization Management Journal, 2009*(3), 16-26. Retrieved April 2, 2014 from EBSCOhost database.

Groves, K. S. & LaRocca, M. A. (2011). An empirical study of leader ethical values, transformational and transactional leadership, and follower attitudes toward corporate social responsibility. *Journal of Business Ethics, 103*(4), 511-528. Retrieved January 2, 2012 from EBSCOhost database.

Grummom, P. T. H. (2010). Trends: In higher education. *Planning for Higher Education, 38*(3), 51-59. Retrieved December 26, 2012 from ProQuest database.

Hamstra, M. R. W., Van Yperen, N. W., Wisse, B., & Sassenberg, K. (2011). Transformational-transactional leadership styles and followers' regulatory focus:
Fit reduces followers' turnover intentions. *Journal of Personnel Psychology, 10*(4), 182-186. Retrieved January 2, 2012 from EBSCOhost database.

Hancock, C. S. (2008). *The effects of leadership in veterinary hospitals on employee Satisfaction and culture* (Doctoral Dissertation). Available from ProQuest Dissertations and Theses database. (UMI No. 3394577)

Handsome, J. D. (2009). *The relationship between leadership style and job satisfaction* (Doctoral Dissertation). Available from ProQuest Dissertations and Theses database. (UMI No. 3379818)

Hargis, M. B. & Bradley III, D. B. (2011). Strategic human resource management in small and growing firms: Aligning valuable resources. *Academy of Strategic Management Journal, 10*(2), 105-125. Retrieved January 28, 2012 from ProQuest database.

Harrison, R., & Stokes, H. (1992). *Diagnosing organizational culture.* San Francisco:Jossey-Bass.

Hasan, S. A. & Subhani, M. I. (2011). Managerial social wisdom: A major facet for employee turnover intentions, work commitments and manager-subordinate relationships. *European Journal of Economics, Finance & Administrative Sciences, 40*, 132 – 137. Retrieved March 18, 2013 from EBSCOhost database.

Hearney, E. & Gerbert, D. (2009). Managing diversity and enhancing team outcomes: The promise of transformation leadership. *Journal of Applied Psychology, 94*(1),7-89. Retrieved April 3, 2014 from ProQuest database.

Hinkin, T. R. & Schriesheim, C.A. (2008). An examination of 'nonleadership': From laissez-faire leadership to leader reward omission and punishment. *Journal of Applied Psychology, 93*(6), 1,234-1,248. Retrieved January 28, 2012 from ProQuest database.

Hogan, R. & Kaiser, R. B. (2008). Quality control: Why leaders needs to understand personality. *Leadership in Action, 28*(5), 3-7. Retrieved February 20, 2011 from EBSCOhost database.

Hsu, C. (2007). *Employees' perception of manager' leadership style, employees' motivation levels, and job satisfaction in Mainland China and Taiwan* (Doctoral Dissertation). Available from ProQuest Dissertations and Theses database. (UMI No. 3286902)

Huseman, R. C., Hatfield, J. D., & Edwards, W. (1987). A new perspective on equity theory: The equity sensitivity construct. *Academy of Management Review*, 12(2), 222-234. Retrieved January 2, 2012 from EBSCOhost database.

Introduction to SAS. UCLA: Statistical Consulting Group. Retrieved August 13, 2013 from http://www.ats.ucla.edu/stat/sas/notes2/ (accessed November 24, 2007).

Jain, R. & Premkumar, R. (2010). Management styles, productivity & adaptability of human resources: An empirical study. *Indian Journal of Industrial Relations, 46*(2), 328-344. Retrieved June 19, 2011from EBSCOhost database.

Jernigan, I. E., & Beggs, J. M. (2005). An examination of satisfaction with my supervisor and organizational commitment. *Journal of Applied Psychology*, 35, 2171-2192. Retrieved July 20, 2013 from EBSCOhost database.

Jex, S. M. & Britt, T. W. (2008). *Organizational psychology: A scientist-practitioner approach (2ⁿᵈ ed.).* Hoboken, NJ; John Wiley & Sons. Johnson, B. & Christensen (2012). *Education Research: Quantitative, Qualitative, and Mixed Approaches* (4ᵗʰ ed). Thousand Oaks, CA: SAGE Publications, Inc.

Jones, D. (2010). Getting the (survey) monkey off your back: Considerations for using an increasingly common data collection tool. *Traumatic Stress Points, 24*(6), 2-4. Retrieved November 27, 2011from EBSCOhost database.

Jones, D. & Rudd, R. (2008). *Transactional, transformational, or laissez-faire leadership: An assessment of college of agriculture academic program leaders' (deans) leadership styles, 49*(2), 88-97. Retrieved June 29, 2013from ProQuest database.

Kamarul, Z. B. A. (2008). Relationship between leader-subordinate personality congruence and performance and satisfaction in the UK. *Leadership & Organization Development Journal, 29*(5), 396-411. Retrieved January 1, 2012 from EBSCOhost database.

Kanji, G. K. (2008). Leadership is prime: How do you measure leadership excellence? *Total Quality Management & Business Excellence, 19*(4), 417-427. Retrieved April 5, 2014 from EBSCOhost database.

Kanste, O., Miettunen, J., & Kynga, S. H. (2007). Psychometric properties of the Multifactor Leadership Questionnaire among nurses. *Journal of Advanced Nursing, 57*(2), 201-212. Retrieved March 25, 2012 from EBSCOhost database.

Katz, P. (2004). *The human side of managing technological innovation (2nd ed.).* New York: Oxford.

Kedsuda, L. & Ogunlana, S. O. (2008). Performance and leadership outcome correlates to leadership styles and subordinate commitment. *Engineering, Construction, and Architectural Management, 15*(2), 164-184. Retrieved December 26, 2012 from ProQuest database.

Kéne, H. & Leenders, M. (2010). Burnout and older workers' intentions to retire. *International Journal of Manpower, 31*(3), 306-321. Retrieved February 28, 2013 from ProQuest database.

Kezar, A. & Eckel, P. (2008). Advancing diversity agendas on campus: examining transactional and transformational presidential leadership. *International Journal of Leadership in Education, 11*(4), 379-405. Retrieved April 14, 2009 from ProQuest database.

Kiger, G. (2008). Sociologist as dean and dean as sociologist. *American Sociologist, 39*(2/3), 110-113. Retrieved May 24, 2009 from EBSCOhost database.

Kim, Y. (2009). Validation of psychometric research instruments: The case of Information science. *Journal of the American Society for Information Science & Technology, 60*(6), 1,178-1,191. Retrieved January 19, 2013 from EBSCOhost database.

Kirkman, M. (2004). *Leadership style of community college department chairs and the effects of faculty job satisfaction* (Doctoral Dissertation). Available from ProQuest Dissertations and Theses database. (UMI No. 3164520)

Kleingeld, A., Van Mierlo, H., & Arends, L. (2011). The effect of goal setting on group performance: A meta-analysis. *Journal of Applied Psychology, 96*(6), 1289-1304. Retrieved January 3, 2012 from EBSCOhost database.

Lange, D. J. (2008). *A correlational analysis of job satisfaction and intent to turnover in a community college organization* (Doctoral Dissertation). Available from ProQuest Dissertations and Theses database. (UMI No. 3322890)

Loghmani, A., Golshiri, P., Zamani, A., Kheirmand, M., & Jafari, N. (2013). Musculoskeletal symptoms and job satisfaction among office-workers: a cross- sectional study from Iran. *Acta Medica Academica, 42*(1), 46-54. Retrieved April 5, 2014 from EBSCOhost database.

Long, J. D. (2004). *Factors that influence nurse attrition: An analysis of the relationship between supervisor leadership style and subordinate job satisfaction* (Doctoral Dissertation). Available from ProQuest Dissertations and Theses database. (UMI No. 3147190)

Lockwood, M. A. (2008). *The relationship of self-efficacy, perceptions of supervisor leadership styles and blue-collar employee engagement* (Doctoral Dissertation). Available from ProQuest Dissertations and Theses database. (UMI No. 3302638)

Lu, Q. & Botha, B. (2006). Process development: a theoretical framework. *International Journal of Production Research, 44*(15), 2,977-2,996. Retrieved January 4, 2013 from ProQuest database.

Mansell, A., Brough, P., & Cole, K. (2006). Stable predictors of job satisfaction, psychological strain, and employee retention: An evaluation of organizational change within the New Zealand customs service. *International Journal of Stress Management, 13*(1), 84-107. Retrieved April 3, 2014 from ProQuest database.

Mardanov, I., Sterrett, J., & Baker, J. (2007). Satisfaction with supervision and member job satisfaction in Leader-Member Exchange: An empirical study in the restaurant industry. *Journal of Applied Management and Entrepreneurship, 12*(3), 37-56. Retrieved January 2, 2013 from ProQuest database.

Mark, G. & Smith, A. P. (2012). Effects of occupational stress, job characteristics, coping, and attributional style on the mental health and job satisfaction of university employees. *Anxiety, Stress & Coping, 25*(1), 63-78. Retrieved April 5, 2014 from EBSCOhost database.

Mast, M. S., Jonas, K., Cronauer, C. K., & Darioly, A. (2012). *Journal of Applied Social Psychology, 42*(5), 1043-1068. Retrieved April 5, 2014 from EBSCOhost database.

McCall Jr., M.W. & Hollenbeck, G. P. (2008). Developing the expert leader. *People & Strategy, 31*(1), 20-28. Retrieved April 2, 2014 from EBSCOhost database.

McNair, D. E., Duree, C. A., & Ebbers, L. (2011). If I knew then what I know now: Using the leadership competencies developed by the American Association of Community Colleges to prepare community college presidents. *Community College Review, 39*(1), 3-25. Retrieved January 1, 2013 from ProQuest database.

Mehta, S. & Maheshwari, G. C. (2013). Consequence of toxic leadership on employee job satisfaction and organizational commitment. *Journal of Contemporary Management Research, 8*(2), 1-23. Retrieved April 5, 2014 from EBSCOhost database.

Mochama, V. K. (2014). The relationship between allocations of equal employee benefits and employee job satisfaction and performance at the Kenya Pipeline Company, Kenya. *Journal of Emerging Trends in Economics and Management Sciences, 4*(2), 262-267. Retrieved April 3, 2014 from ProQuest database.

Mohr, R. D. & Zoghi, C. (2008). High-involvement work design and job satisfaction. *Industrial & Labor Relations Review, 61*(3), 275-296. Retrieved April 5, 2014 from EBSCOhost database.

Mor Barak, M. E., Travis, D., Pyun, H., & Xie, B. (2009). The impact of supervision on worker outcomes: A meta-analysis. *Social Service Review*, *83*(1), 33. Retrieved July 20, 2013 from EBSCOhost database.

Morgan, D. A. (2005). *What steps can a community college take to positively impact employee job satisfaction: A case study* (Doctoral Dissertation). Available from ProQuest Dissertations and Theses database. (UMI No. 3174325)

Munby, S. (2008). Building the perfect team: Leadership in the twenty-first century. *Education Review, 21*(1), 31-38. Retrieved April 5, 2014 from EBSCOhost database.

Murillo, R. (2008). *The relationships between Community Health Workers managers' leadership behavior and CHW's perception of their manager's effectiveness, CHWs' effort, and satisfaction* (Doctoral Dissertation). Available from ProQuest Dissertations and Theses database. (UMI No. 3339610)

Negussie, N. & Demissie, A. (2013). Relationship between leadership styles of nurse managers and nurses' job satisfaction in Jimma University specialized hospital. *Ethiop J. Health Science, 23*(1), 49-58. Retrieved April 13, 2014 from EBSCOhost database.

Neufeld, D. J., Wan, Z., & Fang, Y. (2010). Remote leadership, communication effectiveness and leader performance. *Group Decision and Negotiation, 19*(3), 227-246. Retrieved January 1, 2012 from EBSCOhost database.

Neuman, W. L. (2003). *Social research methods (5th ed.).* Upper Saddle River, NJ: Prentice Hall.

Nicholson, J. L. (2003). *An exploration of the ability to predict student achievement from leadership behaviors, teacher job satisfaction, and socioeconomic status* (Doctoral Dissertation). Available from ProQuest Dissertations and Theses database. (UMI No. 3083806)

Nicolaidou, M. & Petridou, A. (2011). Evaluation of Continuous Professional Development (CDP) programs: challenges and implications for leaders and leadership development. *School Effectiveness & School Improvement, 22*(1), 51- 85. Retrieved April 16, 2012 from EBSCOhost database.

Norris, E. A. (2009). Leadership: Cultivating people skills. *Review of Business Research, 9*(4), 67-83. Retrieve May 24, 2010 from EBSCOhost database.

Northouse, P. G. (2010). *Leadership: Theory and practice (5ᵗʰ ed.).* Thousand Oaks, CA: Sage.

Ozbaran, Y. (2010). *The relationship between Turkish traffic enforcement officers' job satisfaction and officers' perception of their leaders' leadership styles* (Doctoral Dissertation). Available from ProQuest Dissertations and Theses database. (UMI No. 3421480)

Papalexandis, N. & Galanaki, E. (2009). Leadership's impact on employee engagement: Differences among entrepreneurs and professional CEOs. *Leadership & Organization Development Journal, 30*(4), 365-385. Retrieved December 27, 2012 from ProQuest database.

Patel, S. N. (2013). Have we built the committee? Advancing leadership development in the U. S. labor movement. *WorkingUSA, 16*(1), 113-142. Retrieved April 5, 2014 from EBSCOhost database.

Philippe, K. & Mullin, C. M. (2011). *Community college estimated growth: Fall 2010.* American Association of Community Colleges: Washington, DC

Pryor, M. G., Humphreys, J. H., Oyler, J., Taneja, S., & Toombs, L. A. (2011). The legitimacy and efficacy of current organizational theory: An analysis. *International Journal of Management, 28*(4), 209-222. Retrieved January 1, 2013 from ProQuest database.

Ram, P., & Prabhakar, G. (2010). Leadership styles and perceived organizational politics as predictors of work related outcomes. *European Journal of Social Science, 15*(1), 40-55. Retrieved July 20, 2013 from EBSCOhost database.

Rama Devi, V. & Nagini, A (2013). Work-life balance and burnout as predictors of job satisfaction in private banking sector. *Skyline Business Journal, 9*(1), 50-53. Retrieved April 5, 2014 from EBSCOhost database.

Ramsey, M. H. (2010). How terminology and definitions in analytical geochemistry can help or hinder the development of new ideas. *Geostandards & Geoanalytical Research, 34*(4), 317-324. Retrieved January 4, 2013 from ProQuest database.

Ratna, R. & Chawla, S. (2012). Key factors of retention and retention strategies in telecom sector. *Global Management Review, 6*(3), 35-46. Retrieved April 2, 2014 from EBSCOhost database.

Reille, A. & Kezar, A. (2010). Balancing the pros and cons of community college "grow- your-own" Leadership programs. *Community College Review, 38*(1), 59-81. Retrieved December 26, 2012 from ProQuest database.

Riaz, M. N., Anis-ul-Haque, M., & Hassan, B. (2009). Role of individual and Organization factors in leadership. *Pakistan Journal of Psychology, 40*(2). Retrieved April 3, 2014 from ProQuest database.

Riaz, T., Muhammad, U. A., & Hassan, I. (2011). Impact of transformational leadership style on affective employees' commitment: An empirical study of banking sector in Islamad (Pakistan). *The Journal of Commerce, 3*(1), 43. Retrieved February 28, 2013 from ProQuest database.

Riggs, J. (2009). Leadership for tomorrow's community colleges. *The Community College Enterprise, 15*(2), 27-38. Retrieved January 1, 2013 from ProQuest database.

Rosser, V. J., & Townsend, B. K. (2006). Determining public 2-year college faculty's intent to leave: An empirical model. *The Journal of Higher Education, 77*, 125-147. Retrieved January 2, 2013 from UOP University Library database.

Rowe, J. (2006). Non-defining leadership. *Kybernetes, 35*(10), 1528. Retrieved October 4, 2010 from ProQuest database.

Sabri, H. A. (2012). Re-examination of Hofstede's work value orientations on perceived leadership styles in Jordan. *International Journal of Commerce & Management, 22*(3), 202-218. Retrieved April 3, 2014 from ProQuest database.

Sadeghi, A. & Pihie, Z. A. L. (2012). *Transformational leadership and its predictive effects on leadership effectiveness, 3*(7), 186-197. Retrieved June 29, 2013 from ProQuest database.

Sahaya, N. (2012). A learning organization as a mediator of leadership style and firm's financial performance. *International Journal of Business and Management, 7*(14), 96-113. Retrieved April 3, 2014 from ProQuest database.

Salkind, N. J. (2006). *Exploring research (6th ed.)* Upper Saddle River, NJ: Prentice Hall.

Saniewski, L. L. (2011). *The impact of leadership on employee retention* (Doctoral Dissertation). Available from ProQuest Dissertations and Theses database. (UMI No. 3462491)

Sawyer, J. O. IV (2008). *The impact of job satisfaction on the career trajectory of community college administrators in Michigan* (Doctoral Dissertation). Available from ProQuest Dissertations and Theses database. (UMI No. 3335389)

Schermerhorn, J. R., Hunt, J. G., & Osborn, R. N. (2008). *Organizational Behavior (10th ed.)* Hoboken, NJ: John Wiley & Sons, Inc.

Schweer, M., Assimakopoulos, D., Cross, R., & Thomas, R. J. (2012). Building a well-networked organization. *MIT Sloan Magament Review, 53*(2), 35-42. Retrieved January 28, 2012 from ProQuest database.

Shibru, B. & Darshan, G. (2011). Transformational leadership and its relationship with subordinate satisfaction with the leader (The case of leather industry in Ethiopia). *Interdisciplinary Journal of Contemporary Research in Business, 3*(5), 686-697. Retrieved March 25, 2012 from EBSCOhost database.

Silverthrone, C. (2004). The impact of organizational cultural and person-organization fit on organizational commitment and job satisfaction in Taiwan. *Leadership & Organization Development Journal, 25*(7/8). Retrieved January 1, 2013 from ProQuest database.

Silverthorne, C. & Ting-Hsin, W. (2001). Situational leadership style as a predictor of success and productivity among Taiwanese business organizations. *The Journal of Psychology, 135*(4), 399-412. Retrieved January 1, 2013 from ProQuest database.

Sirkis, J. E. (2011). Development of leadership skills in community college department chairs. *The Community College Enterprise, 17*(2), 46-61. Retrieved January 1, 2012 from EBSCOhost database.

Smith, P. (2008). Empirical research. *Empirical Research – Research Starters Education*, 1.1. Retrieved September 19, 2011 from EBSCOhost database.

Söderström, M., Jeding, K., Ekstedt, M., Perski, A., & Akerstedt, T. (2012). Insufficient sleep predicts clinical burnout. *Journal of Occupational Health*

Psychology, *17*(2), 175-183. Retrieved March 3, 2013 from EBSCOhost database.

Soieb, A. Z. M., Othman, J., & D'Silva, J. L. (2013). The effects of perceived leadership styles and organizational citizenship behavior on employee engagement: The mediating role of conflict management. *International Journals of Business and Management, 8*(8), 91-99. Retrieved April 3, 2014 from ProQuest database.

Spector, P. E. (1997). *Job satisfaction: Application, assessment, causes, and consequences (Advance topics in organizational behavior).* Thousand Oaks, CA: Sage.

Stanford, P. (2014). Leadership is influence. *Accountancy, SA,* 16. Retrieved April 3, 2014 from ProQuest database.

Staw, B. M. & Cohen-Charash, Y. (2005). The dispositional approach to job satisfaction: More than a mirage, but not yet an oasis. *Journal of Organizational Behavior, 26*(1), 59-78. Retrieved January 1, 2013 from ProQuest database.

Stiefel, R. H. (2012). Accreditation news and views: The importance of leadership in HTM programs. *Biomedical Instrumentation & Technology, 46*(4), 294-297. Retrieved April 3, 2014 from ProQuest database.

Strom, S. L., Sanchez, A. A., & Downey-Schilling, J. (2011). Inside – outside: Finding future community college leaders. *The Community College Enterprise, 17*(1). Retrieved January 1, 2013 from ProQuest database.

Successful Supervisor (2012). What leadership style works best for you? *Successful Supervisor, 17*(9), 1-2. Retrieved April 5, 2014 from EBSCOhost database.

Sullivan, E. M. (2012). *A correlational study of perceived transformational leadership styles and job satisfaction among social workers* (Doctoral Dissertation). Available from ProQuest Dissertations and Theses database. (UMI No. 3514795)

Sullivan, P. (2010). What is affordable community college tuition?: Part II. *Community College Journal of Research & Practice, 34*(9). Retrieved April 2, 2014 from EBSCOhost database.

Sutton, R. I. (2010). Why good bosses tune in to their people. *McKinsey Quarterly, 3,* 86-95. Retrieved February 28, 2013 from EBSCOhost database.

Sypawka, W., Mallett, W., & McFadden, C. (2010). Leadership styles of community college academic deans. *The Community College Enterprise, 16*(1), 63-73. Retrieved December 26, 2012 from ProQuest database.

Tanoe, C. B. (2010). *Determining the effects of attrition on leadership competency and organization effectiveness: A quantitative study* (Doctoral Dissertation). Available From ProQuest Dissertations and Theses database. (UMI No. 3446508)

Taylor, R. G. & Lynham, S. A. (2013). Systemic leadership for socio-political stewardship. *South African Journal of Business Management, 44*(1), 87-99. Retrieved April 5, 2014 from EBSCOhost database.

Thomas, D. & Au, K. (2002). The effect of cultural differences on behavioral responses to low job satisfaction. *Journal of International Business Studies, 33*(2). Retrieved April 5, 2014 from EBSCOhost database.

Tilleman, S. (2012). Is employee organizational commitment related to firm environmental sustainability? *Journal of Small Business and Entrepreneurship, 25*(4), 417-431, 534. Retrieved March 3, 2013 from ProQuest database.

Üstüner, M. (2009). Teachers' organizational commitment scale: *A validity and reliability study,10(1)*, 1-17, Retrieved on July 25, 2013 from EBSCOhost database.

Valdiserri, G. A. & Wilson, J. L. (2010). The study of leadership in small business organizations: Impact on profitability and organizational success. *The Entrepreneurial Executive, 15*, 47-71. Retrieved April 3, 2014 from ProQuest database.

Valentine, D. (2011). Maintaining organization culture through leadership succession planning. *Frankin Business & Law Journal, 4*, 103-109. Retrieved April 15, 2012 from EBSCOhost database.

van der Doef, M., Mbazzi, F. B., & Verhoeven, C. (2012). Job conditions, job satisfaction, somatic complaints and burnout among East African nurses. *Journal of Clinical Nursing, 11*(12), 1763-1775. Retrieved April 5, 2014 from EBSCOhost database.

Vega, W., Yglesias, K., & Murray, J. P. (2010). Recruiting and mentoring minority faculty members. *New Directions for Community College, 2010*(152), 49-55. Retrieved April 2, 2014 from EBSCOhost database.

Vrba, M. (2007). Emotional intelligence skills and leadership behavior in a sample of South African first-line managers. *Management Dynamics, 16*(2), 25-35. Retrieved April 3, 2014 from ProQuest database.

Wang, J., Tolson, H., Chiang, T., & Huang, T. (2010). An exploratory factor analysis of workplace learning, job satisfaction, and organizational commitment in small to midsize enterprises in Taiwan. *Human Resource Development International, 13*(2), 147-163. Retrieved March 25, 2012 from EBSCOhost database.

Warrick, D. D. (2011). The urgent need for skilled transformational leaders: Integrating transformational leadership and organization development. *Journal of Leadership, Accountability and Ethics, 8*(5), 11-26. Retrieved January 1, 2012 from EBSCOhost database.

Washburn, T. (2012). A correlational analysis of online learning and the transformational leadership style. *The Business Review, Cambridge, 20*(1), 56-61. Retrieved April 3, 2014 from ProQuest database.

Weiss, D. J., Dawis, R. V., England, G. W., & Lofquist, L. H. (1967). *Manual for the Minnesota Satisfaction Questionnaire.* Minnesota Studies in Vocational Rehabilitation: (Whole Number: xxii).

Wilson, D. M. (2010). The hiring game: Reshaping community college practices. *Community College Review, 37*(4), 371-373. Retrieved January 1, 2012 from EBSCOhost database.

Wood, R. D. (2010). *Correlation of conductor leadership style, musician employment status, organizational participation to orchestra musician job satisfaction* (Doctoral Dissertation). Available from ProQuest Dissertations and Theses database. (UMI No. 3488630)

Wood, V. R. (1994). Key components in product management success (and failure): A model of product managers' job performance and job satisfaction in the turbulent 1990s and beyond. *The Journal of Product and Brand Management, 19.* Retrieved January 1, 2013 from ProQuest database.

Workman, T. & Cleveland-Innes, M. (2012). Leadership, personal transformation, and management. *International Review of Research in Open and Distance Learning, 13*(4), 313-3222. Retrieved April 5, 2014 from EBSCOhost database.

Wu, F. Y. (2009). The relationship between leadership styles and foreign English teachers job satisfaction in Adult English Cram Schools: Evidences in Taiwan. *Journal of American Academy of Business, Cambridge, 14*(2), 75-82. Retrieved January 5, 2013 from ProQuest database.

Yin-Fah, B. C., Yeoh, S. F., Lim, C., & Osman, S. (2010). An exploratory study on turnover intention among private sector employees. *International Journal of Business & Management, 5*(8), 57 -64. Retrieved March 25, 2012 from EBSCOhost database.

Yukl, G. (1989). Managerial leadership: A review of theory and research. *Journal of Management, 15*(2), 251-289. Retrieved October 10, 2010 from EBSCOhost database.

Zeffane, R., Tipu, S. A., & Ryan, J. C. (2011). Communication, commitment & trust: Exploring the triad. *International Journal of Business and Management, 6*(6), 77- 87. Retrieved March 3, 2013 from ProQuest database.

Zeiss, T. (2010). Masters of our own destiny. *Community College Journal, 80*(4), 24-25. Retrieved April 2, 2014 from EBSCOhost database.

Zopiatis, A. & Constani, P. (2012). Extraversion, openness, and conscientiousness. *Leadership & Organization Development Journal, 33*(1), 86-104. Retrieved April 3, 2014 from ProQuest database.

Appendix A

Premises, Recruitment, and Name (PRN) Use Permission Form

 University of Phoenix®

PREMISES, RECRUITMENT AND NAME (PRN) USE PERMISSION

Dallas County Community College District

Name of Facility, Organization, University, Institution, or Association

☒ I hereby authorize _Ruben Johnson_ , a student of University of Phoenix, to use the premises (facility identified below) to conduct a study entitled Perceived Leadership Style and Job Satisfaction: Analysis of Instructional and Support Department Managers in Community Colleges.

☒ I hereby authorize _Ruben Johnson_ , a student of University of Phoenix, to recruit subjects for participation in a conduct a study entitled Perceived Leadership Style and Job Satisfaction: Analysis of Instructional and Support Department Managers in Community Colleges.

☒ I hereby authorize _Ruben Johnson_ , a student of University of Phoenix, to use the name of the facility, organization, university, institution, or association identified above when publishing results from the study entitled Perceived Leadership Style and Job Satisfaction: Analysis of Instructional and Support Department Managers in Community Colleges.

_____   7/9/2012

Dr. Wright Lassiter   Date

Chancellor

1601 South Lamar, Dallas, Texas 75202

Appendix B

● ● ●

DCCCD IRB Approval Letter

Office of Institutional Research
Dallas County Community College District

February 05, 2104

From: Dallas County Community College District
       Institutional Review Board
       Dr. Richard K. Plott, Chair
       1601 South Lamar Street
       Dallas, Texas 75215-1816
       214.378.1834 Office
       richardplott@dcccd.edu

To: Mr. Ruben Johnson
       Doctoral Candidate
       University of Phoenix
       Student ID – 3100906627

RE: DCCCD IRB Approval

Mr. Johnson,

Thank you for submitting the required documentation for review by the Dallas County Community College District – Institutional Review Board. After careful consideration of this request, the committee has approved for the research to be conducted according to the guidelines proposed in the application. The project start date has been itemized as 12/01/13; with a completion date itemized as 02/28/14. Should the research not be completed by the "Research Study Timeline" notated in the application; an additional review will be required. Our committee will reconvene in April 2014 for any request received during the first quarter of the current calendar year, with results sent to applicants at the end of that month.

There are not additional items required and the research may begin immediately. All colleges within the DCCCD will honor the decision of the IRB Committee; however, each college may vary in the resources available for you to utilize at their location. Thank you and best wishes throughout your candidacy.

Respectfully,

Dr. Richard K. Plott,
IRB Committee Chair

Appendix C

Introductory E-Mail

Introductory E-Mail to Survey Participants

Dear Colleague:

I am a doctoral student at the University of Phoenix working on my dissertation entitled Perceived Leadership Style and Job Satisfaction: Analysis of Instructional and Support Departments in Community Colleges.

The purpose of this quantitative correlation study is to measure the relationships between the subordinate's perceived leadership style of the instructional or support leaders and the level of the subordinate's job satisfaction.

A SurveyMonkey© website will be used to gather data and information to complete the current study. The estimate time for completing the survey is 20 - 22 minutes. Your participation will involve the completion of two survey instruments and a demographic survey questionnaire.

The Minnesota Satisfaction Questionnaire Short Form, 1977 (MSQ) developed by Weiss, Dawis, England, and Lofquist (1977), will measure the job satisfaction of the instructional department employees.

The MSQ survey will consist of 20 questions, and the purpose of this survey is to measure an employee's level of satisfaction (very satisfied, satisfied, neither satisfied nor dissatisfied, dissatisfied, or very dissatisfied) with his or her job (dependent variable). The MSQ survey will take approximately 3 - 5 minutes to complete this survey.

The Multifactor Leadership Questionnaire Form 5X Short, 3rd ed. (MLQ), developed by Burns (1978) and refined by Bass and Avolio (2004), will define the leadership styles (independent variable). The MLQ will consist of 45 questions and the purpose of this survey is to identify the perceived leadership style of a leader (transformational, transactional, and laissez-faire) by the subordinate. It will take approximately 10 - 15 minutes to complete this survey. Your answers to these surveys are neither right nor wrong, and all responses will remain confidential.

The demographic survey covers questions pertaining to the employees, such as: sex, age, ethnicity, education level, job title, length of employment, employment status, and department. The demographic survey will take approximately 1 - 2 minutes to complete.
Your participation in this study is voluntary.

If you choose not to complete the surveys, you can withdraw from the study at any time; you can withdraw without penalty or loss of benefit to yourself. The results of the research study may be published. The results of the study will be collected and analyzed in aggregate format. In this research, there are no foreseeable risks to you. Although there may be no direct benefit to you, participation in the study could contribute to the academic and leadership knowledge related to job satisfaction.

By you completing the surveys on the SurveyMonkey© website indicate that you understand the nature of this study, risks, and confidentiality of responses.

If you have any questions concerning the research study, please call at 972-860-8161 or e-mail me at rjohnson@dcccd.edu.

Thank you for your consideration and willingness to participate in this study.

Sincerely,
Ruben Johnson
Doctoral Student
University of Phoenix
School of Advance Studies

Here is a link to the survey: https://www.surveymonkey.com/s/87LBW9M

This link is uniquely tied to this survey and your email address. Please do not forward this message.

Thanks for your participation!

r/s
Ruben Johnson, MBA, BS, AGS
Executive Dean
Business & Technology Division
Cedar Valley College
3030 N. Dallas Avenue, B-201
Lancaster, TX 75134
rjohnson@dcccd.edu
972-860-8161 (Office)
972-860-8052 (Fax)

Appendix D

* * *

Demograhic Sheet

Today's Date

_____20____

1. Gender: ☐ Male   ☐ Female

2. Age:

    18-32 _____ 33-42 _____ 43-52 _____ 53-60 _____ 60+ _____

3. Ethnicity:

    Caucasian ___ Black ___ Hispanic ___ American Indian ___ Other ___

4. Education Level:

    GED ___ High Diploma ___ Bachelor's ___ Master's ___ Doctorate ___

5. What is the title of your present job?

    _____

6. How long have you worked for DCCCD?

    _____ years _____ months

7. Employment Status:

    Administrator – Full time ___ Administrator – Part time ___ Faculty – Full time ___

    Faculty – Part time ___ PSS – Full time ___ PSS – Part time ___

8. What department do you work in?

    Instructions ___ Student Services ___

Appendix E

Multifactor Leadership Questionnaire

For use by Ruben Johnson only. Received from Mind Garden, Inc. on December 29, 2011

Multifactor Leadership Questionnaire
Rater Form

Name of Leader: _____Date: _____

This questionnaire is used to describe the leadership style of the above-mentioned individual as you perceive it. Answer all items on this answer sheet. **If an item is irrelevant, or if you are unsure or do not know the answer, leave the answer blank.** Please answer this questionnaire anonymously.

Important (necessary for processing): Which best describes you?

___ I am at a higher organizational level than the person I am rating.

___ The person I am rating is at my organizational level.

___ I am at a lower organizational level than the person I am rating.

___ Other than the above.

Forty-five descriptive statements are listed on the following pages. Judge how frequently each statement fits the person you are describing. Use the following rating scale:

Not at all	Once in a while	Sometimes	Fairly often	Frequently, if not always
0	1	2	3	4

The Person I Am Rating. . .

1. Provides me with assistance in exchange for my efforts.............. 0 1 2 3 4
2. *Re-examines critical assumptions to question whether they are appropriate 0 1 2 3 4
3. Fails to interfere until problems become serious 0 1 2 3 4
4. Focuses attention on irregularities, mistakes, exceptions, and deviations from standards.. 0 1 2 3 4
5. Avoids getting involved when important issues arise.................. 0 1 2 3 4
6. *Talks about his/her most important values and beliefs.............. 0 1 2 3 4
7. Is absent when needed 0 1 2 3 4
8. *Seeks differing perspective when solving problems.................... 0 1 2 3 4
9. *Talks optimistically about the future 0 1 2 3 4
10. *Instills pride in me for being associated with him/her 0 1 2 3 4
11. Discusses in specific terms who is responsible for achieving performance targets... 0 1 2 3 4
12. Waits for things to go wrong before taking action 0 1 2 3 4
13. *Talks enthusiastically about what needs to be accomplished 0 1 2 3 4
14. *Specifies the importance of having a strong sense of purpose...... 0 1 2 3 4
15. *Spends time teaching and coaching 0 1 2 3 4

Continued •

Not at all	Once in a while	Sometimes	Fairly often	Frequently, if not always
0	1	2	3	4

16. Makes clear what one can expect to receive when performance goals are achieved 0 1 2 3 4

17. Shows that he/she is a firm believer in "If it ain't broke, don't fix it 0 1 2 3 4

18. *Goes beyond self-interest for the good of the group............... 0 1 2 3 4

19. *Treats me as an individual rather than just as a member of a group 0 1 2 3 4

20. Demonstrates that problems must become chronic before taking action... 0 1 2 3 4

21. *Acts in ways that builds my respect... 0 1 2 3 4

22. Concentrates his/her full attention on dealing with mistakes, complaints, and failures....................................... 0 1 2 3 4

23. *Considers the moral and ethical consequences of decisions 0 1 2 3 4

24. Keeps track of all mistakes 0 1 2 3 4

25. *Displays a sense of power and confidence............................... 0 1 2 3 4

26. *Articulates a compelling vision of the future........................... 0 1 2 3 4

27. Directs my attention toward failures to meet standards............. 0 1 2 3 4

28. Avoids making decisions.. 0 1 2 3 4

29. *Considers me as having different needs, abilities, and aspirations from others... 0 1 2 3 4

30. *Gets me to look at problems from many different angles 0 1 2 3 4

31. *Helps me to develop my strengths... 0 1 2 3 4

32. *Suggests new ways of looking at how to complete assignments 0 1 2 3 4

33. Delays responding to urgent questions 0 1 2 3 4

34. *Emphasizes the importance of having a collective sense of mission 0 1 2 3 4

35. Expresses satisfaction when I meet expectations 0 1 2 3 4

36. *Expresses confidence that goals will be achieved..................... 0 1 2 3 4

37. Is effective in meeting my job-related needs............................. 0 1 2 3 4

38. Uses methods of leadership that are satisfying.......................... 0 1 2 3 4

39. Gets me to do more than I expected to do 0 1 2 3 4
40. Is effective in representing me to higher authority 0 1 2 3 4
41. Works with me in a satisfactory way 0 1 2 3 4
42. Heightens my desire to succeed 0 1 2 3 4
43. Is effective in meeting organizational requirements 0 1 2 3 4
44. Increases my willingness to try harder 0 1 2 3 4
45. Leads a group that is effective 0 1 2 3 4

Appendix F

Permission To Use MLQ Form 5X-Short Instrument

August 13, 2013

Ruben Johnson
981 Holly Lane
Cedar Hill, TX 75104

Dear Ruben Johnson,

This letter is to confirm that you, Ruben Johnson, have purchased via Invoice 25766 (July 17, 2012) and Invoice 26676 (August 9, 2013), a total of 200 Multifactor Leadership Questionnaire (MLQ) RATER ONLY online survey licenses. Based on this purchase, you have Mind Garden's permission (consent), for your research, to administer the MLQ copyrighted instrument via our Mind Garden Transform Online Survey System.

Instrument: *Multifactor Leadership Questionnaire*

Authors: *Bruce Avolio and Bernard Bass*

Copyright: *1995 by Bruce Avolio and Bernard Bass*

Five sample items from this instrument may be reproduced for inclusion in a proposal, thesis, or dissertation. Please note that the five sample items may not represent a complete scale.

The entire instrument may not be included or reproduced at any time in any published material.

Best regards,

Chris Coultas
Mind Garden, Inc.

Appendix G

Minnesota Satisfaction Questionanaire Instrument

minnesota satisfaction questionnaire
(short-form)

Vocational Psychology Research

UNIVERSITY OF MINNESOTA

Copyright 1977

minnesota satisfaction questionnaire

The purpose of this questionnaire is to give you a chance to tell **how you feel about your present job,** what things you are **satisfied** with and what things you are **not satisfied** with.

On the basis of your answers and those of people like you, we hope to get a better understanding of the things people **like and dislike about their jobs.**

On the next page you will find statements about your **present** job.

· Read each statement carefully.

· Decide **how satisfied you feel about the aspect of your job** described by the statement.

Keeping the statement in mind:

— if you feel that your job gives you **more than you expected,** check the box under **"Very Sat."** (Very Satisfied);

— if you feel that your job gives you **what you expected,** check the box under **"Sat."** (Satisfied);

— if you **cannot make up your mind** whether or not the job gives you what you expected, check the box under **"N"** (Neither Satisfied nor Dissatisfied);

— if you feel that your job gives you **less than you expected,** check the box under **"Dissat."** (Dissatisfied);

— if you feel that your job gives you **much less than you expected,** check the box under **"Very Dissat."** (Very Dissatisfied).

· Remember: Keep the statement in mind when deciding **how satisfied you feel about that aspect of your job.**

· Do this for **all** statements. Please answer **every** item.

Be frank and honest. Give a true picture of your feelings about your **present job.**

2

*Ask yourself: How **satisfied** am I with this aspect of my job?*

Very Sat. *means I am very satisfied with this aspect of my job.*

Sat. *means I am satisfied with this aspect of my job.*

N *means I can't decide whether I am satisfied or not with this aspect of my job.*

Dissat. *means I am dissatisfied with this aspect of my job.*

Very Dissat. *means I am very dissatisfied with this aspect of my job.*

On my present job, this is how I feel about . . .	Very Dissat.	Dissat.	N	Sat.	Very Sat.
1. Being able to keep busy all the time	☐	☐	☐	☐	☐
2. The chance to work alone on the job	☐	☐	☐	☐	☐
3. The chance to do different things from time to time	☐	☐	☐	☐	☐
4. The chance to be "somebody" in the community	☐	☐	☐	☐	☐
5. The way my boss handles his/her workers	☐	☐	☐	☐	☐
6. The competence of my supervisor in making decisions	☐	☐	☐	☐	☐
7. Being able to do things that don't go against my conscience	☐	☐	☐	☐	☐
8. The way my job provides for steady employment	☐	☐	☐	☐	☐
9. The chance to do things for other people	☐	☐	☐	☐	☐
10. The chance to tell people what to do	☐	☐	☐	☐	☐
11. The chance to do something that makes use of my abilities	☐	☐	☐	☐	☐
12. The way company policies are put into practice	☐	☐	☐	☐	☐
13. My pay and the amount of work I do	☐	☐	☐	☐	☐
14. The chances for advancement on this job	☐	☐	☐	☐	☐
15. The freedom to use my own judgment	☐	☐	☐	☐	☐
16. The chance to try my own methods of doing the job	☐	☐	☐	☐	☐
17. The working conditions	☐	☐	☐	☐	☐
18. The way my co-workers get along with each other	☐	☐	☐	☐	☐
19. The praise I get for doing a good job	☐	☐	☐	☐	☐
20. The feeling of accomplishment I get from the job	☐	☐	☐	☐	☐
	Very Dissat.	Dissat.	N	Sat.	Very Sat.

3

131

Appendix H

Permission To Use MSQ Short Form Instrument

UNIVERSITY OF MINNESOTA

Twin Cities Campus	*Department of Psychology*	*S/218 Elliott Hall*
	College of Liberal Arts	*75 East River Road*
		Minneapolis, MN 55455
		Office: 612-625-2818
		Fax: 612-626-2079
		www.psych.umn.edu

February 7, 2012

Ruben Johnson
981 Holly Ln
Cedar Hill, TX 75104

Dear Rubin Johnson:

We are pleased to grant you permission to use the Minnesota Satisfaction Questionnaire 1977 short form on a secure web site in your research project as you requested.

Please note that each copy that you make must include the following copyright statement:

Copyright 1977, Vocational Psychology Research
University of Minnesota. Reproduced by permission.

Vocational Psychology Research is currently in the process of revising the MSQ manual and it is very important that we receive copies of your research study results in order to construct new norm tables. Therefore, we would appreciate receiving a copy of your results including 1) Demographic data of respondents, including age, education level, occupation and job tenure; and 2) response statistics including, scale means, standard deviations, reliability coefficients, and standard errors of measurement.

Your providing this information will be an important and valuable contribution to the new MSQ manual. If you have any questions concerning this request, please feel free to call us at 612-625-1367.

Sincerely,

Dr. David J. Weiss, Director
Vocational Psychology Research

Driven to Discover™

Appendix I

● ● ●

Summary of Correlations for Leadership Styles and Job Satisfaction

*S*ummary *of Correlations for Leadership Styles (MLQ-5x) and Job Satisfaction (MSQ) (n = 263)*

	Measure	1	2	3	4	5	6	7	8	9
1.	Overall Satisfaction (O)	1.000								
2.	Intrinsic (I)	.956**	1.000							
3.	Extrinsic (E)	.909**	.763**	1.000						
4.	Transformational (TF)	.721**	.637**	.775**	1.000					
5.	Transactional (TA)	.366**	.305**	.457**	.607**	1.000				
6.	Laissez-faire (LF)	-.650**	-.557**	-.697**	-.766**	-.445**	1.000			
7.	Extra effort (EE)	.111	.083	.135*	.107	.010	-.093	1.000		
8.	Effectiveness (EFF)	.130*	.094	.152*	.135	-.009	-.094	.829**	1.000	
9.	Satisfaction (SAT)	.147*	.100	.184**	.156*	.024	-.120	.830**	.899**	1.000

*Note. N = 263. **p < .01, two-tailed. *p < .05, two-tailed.*